MW00643193

PRAISE FOR THE AUTHORS'
THE SECRET LIFE OF GIRLS

"A tribute to girls, cleverly disguised as humor, and a fount of useful information about them."

Chicago *Tribune*

"Yuckles and chuckles ... filled with enough home truths to keep a whole summer house giggling on a rainy day."

New York *Daily News*

"Funny, penetrating..."

Denver *Post*

"...resurrects the idealized feminine creature whom the feminists have been trying to bury for the last several decades."

Los Angeles *Times*

"Jam-packed with useful tidbits and real answers to the puzzling questions that boys — and men — face every day."

Playboy

"...geniuses..."

Sonya Friedman, *The Sonya Show,*
USA Cable Network

THE GROWN-UP GIRL'S GUIDE TO BOYS

LESLEY DORMEN AND MARK ZUSSMAN

Illustrated by Joel Glassman

BERKLEY BOOKS, NEW YORK

THE GROWN-UP GIRL'S GUIDE TO BOYS

A Berkley Book/published by arrangement with
the authors

PRINTING HISTORY
Berkley trade paperback edition/May 1986

ISBN: 0-425-08667-4

A BERKLEY BOOK ® TM 757,375

Contents

7

THE GROWN-UP GIRL'S GUIDE TO BOYS

How Boys Came Back from the Dead

Whatever ill repute boys began to fall into when they dragged women around by the hair in paleolithic caves, their reputation had never sunk as low as it did in the 1970s, and never before had they joined so fervently in the chorus of voices against them, and never had they found so little to say in their own defense. Reviled by their mothers and their wives and their girlfriends, treated as pariahs by total strangers on the bus, boys, as never before in the past, hung their heads in shame and confessed to their crimes on nationally syndicated talk shows. They confessed to the old crimes of bad spelling, lousy posture, and tracking in mud; and they owned up to brand-new charges of insensitivity, unsupportiveness, and lousy foreplay technique. Every once in a while a boy would find a moment's solace in the example of Thomas Jefferson, Albert Schweitzer, Jesse Owens, or Hugh Downs. But it didn't last. He had come to believe that every male human being was a boy, hence a polluter, a pillager of Third World economies, a violator of library quiet rules, and a mooner. He dreaded quarantine but wondered if it wouldn't be for the greater good of society.

In order to avoid being rounded up, boys turned themselves in for an extended period of rehabilitation. They learned sympathy and baking. They learned which side the fork goes on. They learned to affect a charming uncertainty about whether to hold a door open or just barge on through. They learned that many primitive societies were actually organized as matriarchies and that Jill Clayburgh didn't stay with Alan Bates in *An Unmarried Woman* because she hadn't found *herself* yet. Boys learned all this and more, and still there were traces all over the place. There was the wet towel on the bathroom floor, the phrase, "Good game, huh," the tennis racket strummed as an electric guitar, the Accelerated Cost Recovery System for assets placed in service after December 31, 1980. The stake had been driven through the heart all right, but someone had forgotten to bury the corpse at the crossroads.

Eighteen Heroes and Superheroes That a Boy Can Never Be One Hundred Percent Sure He Isn't

Superman

The Lone Ranger

The Kid

007

The Wild Bunch

The Three Musketeers

King of Comedy

Dawn Patrol

The Seventh Cavalry

The Sixth Fleet

A–Number One

King of the Hill

The Big Cheese

The Lord of Hosts

The Supreme Being

Zeus

God's Gift to Women

The Duke of Earl

Boys and Their Mothers

A boy loves his mother more than any other human being on the face of the earth, and this is why he frequently comes so close to actually calling her on the telephone or even stopping off at the drugstore to get her a Whitman's Sampler, before he eats the dinner she made for him and falls asleep on her couch. It is also why he frequently comes so close to beating her senseless with a table lamp and walling her body up in the basement. In practice, though, a boy rarely goes to either of these extremes. Rather, he expresses his tenderness for her by inquiring into the progress of her arthritis and, because he is so pleased with the exchange, he goes on to try to explain to her the precise meaning of his new job title; she interrupts to wonder what ever happened to that nice Louise who worked with the autistic children and if he's sure he's warm enough in such a thin jacket, and he reverts to his customary monosyllables, his veiled threats, his double entendres, and his muttered asides. A boy feels guilt and remorse for the part he plays in these downhill encounters, and he regularly resolves to put the past in its place and, in the future, work even harder to cement what could become a really pleasant relationship between two reasonable and enlightened adults—or at least between one reasonable and enlightened adult and one lovely person who, through no fault of her own and probably as a result of chemical imbalances in the brain, continues to act as if she knew him when.

Boys and Their Moms

Sometimes a boy will feel full of remorse for the shameful way he's been treating his mother, and sometimes at sea, at war, at summer camp, in front of an overcooked pot roast, in front of a tattoo parlor, or in front of a firing squad, he will make a mental note to pay back the $10,000 she scraped together out of her household monies and loaned him interest-free so that he could open up a combination sushi bar/scuba-instruction center. On such an occasion, a boy will praise his mother to a total stranger for the way she used to hold his head when he vomited, for the way she prepared French toast exactly to his specifications, and for the way she finally learned to fold his socks and organize them in his drawer so that he wouldn't have to call her in to redo it; and he will kick himself for not having appreciated really first-class service when he had it, before moving out into a world of inattentive waiters, unfeeling Chinese laundries, and girlfriends who won't even come and watch when he plays tennis.

How a Boy Keeps Himself from Poking His Father in the Eye

A boy's mother is so blindly admiring of him that she sees him holding a steady course for the Governor's mansion, even if he is already in his mid-thirties and still struggling with a master's in social work and still bringing his laundry home on Tuesday evenings. A boy's father, who is not blindly admiring of a boy at all, believes, by contrast, that he is headed straight for the electric chair and that it is probably only as a result of bumbling police work that he hasn't kept his appointment there already. A father's case against a boy is that he sleeps too much, he thinks that life is one long party, he is monstrously disrespectful, and he refuses to keep his eye on the ball; and, because a father is so expressive of his dissatisfaction, a boy often spends the last few minutes before he drifts off at night planning to knock his father's block off. A boy might someday act on his revenge fantasies, too, except that by the time he's tall enough and heavy enough he has already learned to take out his hostile feelings on golf balls, tennis balls, Andy Rooney, the person who calls up to offer him an opportunity to subscribe to *Time* at the special introductory rate, and dates. A boy also discovers somewhere along the line that he isn't much impressed by disrespect himself and he also doesn't like shiftlessness, skulking, and people who don't know the meaning of a dollar, and he begins to wonder just what it was that had him so teed off at that grand old guy in the first place.

Eighteen Expressions of the Special Bond Between a Boy and His Sister

"Calm down. I'm just going to drive it around the block. I'll be back hours before they get home."

"Just show me the basic steps."

"Here! Catch!"

"I was not looking through your keyhole."

"I've already seen you undressed and I wasn't impressed."

"You've got thirty seconds by the clock to get out of the bathroom or I'm kicking the door down. Thirty, twenty-nine...."

"I might have to kill Aunt Edith, but don't worry, I'll give you twenty-four hours to make your getaway before I say you did it."

"You can trust me. Just close your eyes and hold your breath."

"Say that God is dog spelled backwards and I'll let you out."

"Had enough?"

"Between people like us, taboos don't matter."

"Keep it down. I barely even touched you."

"Tell me exactly what she said about me."

"Act as if you don't know me."

"You're a disgusting slob."

"I don't see how anyone could stand to kiss you."

"You buy it, I don't care what it is, and sign my name. Here's a couple of dollars."

"You're going to marry him? I thought you were going to marry me."

Boys As Brothers

Boys subscribe to a principle of brotherhood so universal that they number, as brothers, not just the guys from Sigma Chi and not just the guys they occupied the student union with but all races, all creeds, and all religions; and, under the influence of alcohol or simply a good, winning softball season, a boy is quite capable of trying to persuade many or most of these brothers to go home with him and stretch a quart of Ballantine, a rancid half-loaf of Wonder bread, a pound of baloney, and a box of Entenmann's cupcakes into dinner for nine. On a normal working day, unfortunately, the principle of universal brotherhood tends to shade into arm's-length neighborliness and that in turn shades into veiled hostility and that into outright enmity and savage power plays which will result in the victor's securing a larger office with more windows and deeper pile carpeting and the loser's having to spend the rest of his life trying to eke out a living as a consultant. As for a boy's actual flesh and blood brother, the one with whom he shares a single biological mother and father, that little snotnose bastard had better return the $150 he borrowed, and he'd better do it the day before yesterday, or else he would be wise to keep his little ratface out of this part of town and stop trying to curry favor by reminiscing about the great times they used to have, twenty years in the past, when they snuck rabbit punches at each other every time their mother had her back turned.

On the Conceit of Boys

Though a girl would be quite impressed enough if a boy simply remembered her birthday and every once in a while invited her out to dinner and carried enough cash on him to pay his part of the bill, a boy would prefer that a girl echo back to him his own self-infatuated conviction that his brilliantly intuitive commentaries have helped her to see the arts in startling new ways, that he is the only sexually proficient male on this part of the globe, that old people, children, and dogs take to him immediately, that it is virtually impossible to understand why he isn't already rich and famous, and that she and her father both stand in awe of him and, furthermore, they wouldn't be a bit surprised to find themselves working for him someday. A boy would not even mind if a girl found discreet ways to tell him some of this stuff explicitly, thereby giving him an opportunity to display his modesty, point out areas in which she exaggerates, and get her to refine her case and explain in precise and accurate detail just what it was she meant when she spoke of his "nice way of handling things." Boys really do think remarkably well of themselves, and their monumental swelled-headedness survives and even thrives on their repeated bobbles and fumbles, their inept comebacks, their failure to get the hang of charades, and their constant vulnerability to the "Do you have Prince Albert in a can?" joke. A boy thinks that any skill for which he lacks a natural aptitude is OK if you want to be a grind, a jock, or a professional plumber or air conditioner repairman but not if you want to make big bucks in equipment leasing and own beachfront property in Malibu.

When a boy occasionally does do something that is large-hearted, noble, and brave, chances are good that he will prefer to slink back into the woodwork rather than hang around, bask in the limelight, collect the cash reward, and accept the thanks of a grateful cat owner. This, however, is not because there is a streak of real modesty underneath all his boasting, bragging, and showing off. More likely, he would simply not like to call too much attention to himself, and in particular he may be concerned that, if his name and his photograph turn up in the newspaper, some reporter with a long memory might dredge up the old stuff about the brontosaurus bones hoax and the publicity might turn out to be a lot more bother than it's worth.

On the Vanity of Boys

Boys would know a lot more about what they look like if they learned to use mirrors as sources of information on a par with world almanacs, eyewitnesses, and maps. But instead boys use mirrors chiefly as audiences. They use mirrors to talk back to their bosses, to mug, to sneer, to try to frighten the bejesus out of themselves, and to engage in drawing and shooting contests with Wyatt Earp, and as a direct result of this boys have no idea at all what they look like. It is also because of their misuse of mirrors that boys regularly forget to clip their nose hairs and that they go out thinking that they look great, or even that they look like trouble, when in fact they look pretty much like the next guy. A boy is indeed so utterly confused and befuddled about his appearance that he will always get a little uncomfortable when a girl confides that she's never had much use for conventionally handsome men anyway, and he will go into his ready alert mode, a step short of full mobilization, if she lets on that he reminds her of Gene Wilder or John Candy—it had been his distinct impression that people were standing out of his way on the street because they were mistaking him for Sam Shepard or Sting. Moreover, despite his occasional dangerous brushes with reality—a friendly hint, for example, that, now that he's maturing, he might want to try a conditioning shampoo or a simple skin moisturizer—a boy will remain doggedly loyal to a hair style that isn't seen much anymore outside the pages of *The National Geographic* and to a daily toilet that consists of a couple of minutes with a deodorant soap strong enough to resuscitate Detroit, and an occasional touch-up with Binaca. A boy will also remain impervious to the argument that it doesn't matter what Pee-Wee Herman does, Bermuda shorts just don't cut it anymore, and he will maintain that the shirt he's wearing isn't a nauseating lime green at all, it's a pale blue his mother used to like him to wear because it brings out the magic in his eyes.

Boys and Hair Loss

When a boy looks into the mirror and catches an unexpected glimpse of his Uncle Bernie, he does not feel a whole lot better to be reminded of how virile and cute Yul Brynner and Telly Savalas are, and neither does it improve his spirits much to be reminded that Robert Duvall won an Academy Award for *Tender Mercies* or that John Malkovich was really outstanding in *Places in the Heart* and *True West*. At any given moment, a boy may indeed feel that he has arrived at the crucial turning point of maximum acceptable hair loss and that, with as little as one more week of further erosion at the present rate, he's either going to have to come up with a pretty strong new line of patter or strike it rich in pork belly futures, or else he might as well wrap himself up neatly in a large plastic bag and throw himself out with the garbage. A boy comes out of a hair loss crisis when some girl he's never even seen before smiles at him in the macaroni aisle, he takes another close look at himself in his bathroom mirror, he discovers an amazing new way of parting his hair, and he convinces himself that he's just bought one more year.

How Boys Keep House

Because it is not essentially in the nature of boys to have a fixed and permanent place of residence, the address a boy sets up at in order to receive his junk mail and jury duty notices will inevitably come to resemble one or more of the environments in which he does feel at home—namely, the barracks, the lair, the kennel, the warehouse, the motel room, or the garage. A boy will always furnish his living quarters for his own purposes, not for guests, but it will not cross his mind that the occasional guest is not as happy as he is to lounge on an unmade bed and drink out of a Saucee shrimp cocktail glass and stare at the ceiling, provided of course that the speakers are in phase and the supply of Dorito chips is sufficient to last through breakfast. This is why, when occasionally in the dead of night he drags back not another dead and abandoned television set and not another junked footlocker, but a girl, and he throws open the door and says, "Voila!" he will be stone-blind to her distress and he will miss entirely how close she comes to actually fleeing. He will also miss the horror she feels for the encrusted silverware, the sodden bathtowel, the rancid kitchen odors, the erotic ashtrays,

and the guy he met once in Colorado, now sleeping semi-permanently in a drug-induced stupor on the living room couch. Six months later, despite her best efforts, he will still not see it, and one day, when she says in a fit of pique, "How can you stand to live this way?" he will answer innocently, "What way?"

Later still, a girl prevails on a boy to move, and he invests vast treasure and energy in converting two thousand square feet of former factory space into an *Architectural Digest* dream of bleached wood floors, walls the color of a celery stalk, ingenious built-ins, and a restaurant-quality stove. It is then that a boy looks around him and feels both domestic bliss and the deep satisfaction of ownership and realizes that this is the home he was meant to live in all along, and he will wonder how a girl with so much intuitive taste and style could leave her makeup out on the imported marble vanity and, with enough walk-in closet space to satisfy Princess Diana, still have him climbing over dumbbells, a pile of dirty laundry, and a dozen shoe boxes just to get to his rowing machine.

Where Boys Hide Things

A boy believes that virtually everything he owns is either precious or incriminating, and this is why he figures that, if he's going to go to the trouble of putting something away, he might as well go the extra half mile and hide it outright. He puts the girlie magazines in the clothes hamper, the dirty underwear in the bottom drawer, the Folkdance Club newsletter under the *Gentlemen's Quarterly*s, and the country house lawn furniture in petty cash, and consequently he can rarely find anything himself. Very early on, hiding ceases to serve any real purpose for a boy and becomes merely reflex; hence, he is likely to go through life putting down a legitimate business lunch with one client as a legitimate business dinner with another client and having no clear idea why. A boy himself can generally be found hiding behind sunglasses, a mustache, and an unlikely story, or, if he is rich and powerful enough, behind a receptionist, a couple of secretaries, and a battery of high-priced lawyers. The only stuff that a boy doesn't hide is the stuff that he means specifically to exhibit, that is, his car, his Kuwait Hilton matchbooks, and his framed letter of commendation from the Springview Manor Home for the Aged for the magic act he performed at the annual Christmas party; and he also leaves out a few false leads in order to keep the curious and the nosy off of the real trail. When a girl asks a boy, "Are you hiding something from me?" he will always look at her incredulously, and he will answer, "Of course not. What could I possibly have to hide?"

Seventeen Things That a Boy Will Never Throw Out Come Hell or High Water

Ninety-eight copies of his high school graduation photograph, two fewer than he had printed up

A photograph of the grandfather he never met, in the uniform of a first lieutenant, playfully holding a dagger between his teeth, in front of the Eiffel Tower, a week and a half before the battle of Château-Thierry

A mailing from the Perth Chamber of Commerce

A deed for one square inch of land somewhere in Alaska

$2.67 (face value) in Indian head pennies

A clipping from his hometown newspaper in which his own name appears in a single sentence with the phrase "dismissed for insufficient evidence," laminated and framed

A copy of the speech he wrote during his unsuccessful bid for the student body presidency, on how he would straighten out the parking problem once and for all and bring in the Rolling Stones to perform at the senior prom

A plastic replica of the St. Louis Gateway Arch, ugly, useless, and utterly without value in cash or trade, shoplifted from a Woolworth's, because it was there

His mother's spaghetti sauce recipe

A letter from John Glenn in response to his inquiry about whether or not you could still be an astronaut if you had measles when you were a kid

The 107 parking tickets he collected during a summer at school in Boston, which, even though he has no intention of paying them, he believes he might get into trouble for throwing out

A baseball autographed by every last member of the 1961 Cleveland Indians, reluctantly turned over by a kid named Tommy, because it was fair, for shooting at the principal with a water pistol, in broad daylight

An amazing picture of a stark-naked girl and a frightened-looking burro, one corner missing, which he found while rummaging idly one afternoon in his father's bottom drawer

A certificate of ministry in the Church of the Divine Spirit of Glendale, California

Plastic chips, stacked

Handcuffs

A carburetor

Where Boys Get the Energy

If the enormous energy of boys could be harnessed and made to do an honest day's work, potholes would always be filled in promptly, garbage would be taken out before it rotted and attracted vermin, lawns would be weed-free, and the concept of corrective maintenance would fade into memory, because everything would always be kept in A-1 condition and tip-top working order. Fortunately, though, for the people who clean up the mess, usually after normal working hours at time and a half, boys do not harness easily and they are not energy-efficient systems. The energy of boys comes in fits and starts; moreover, when boys do get a surge of get-up-and-go, they have an awful time identifying any place to get up and go to. Boys, accordingly, use up a lot of their energy either spinning their wheels, running in place, kicking up dirt, or dribbling, fidgeting, cannonballing, and putting English on things that don't need it, or on wild goose chases or fool's errands, often involving uniformed airline stewardesses who don't even know that a boy exists, with the result that boys will sometimes spend a good part of the afternoon simply letting off steam or taking cold showers. Alternatively, boys will wear themselves out and switch to auxiliary energy sources such as free-floating anxiety or adrenaline, and then they will get to have a funny acrid odor about them and babble unintelligibly and then they will crash.

The world in general, and the authorities in particular, devote a substantial portion of their very limited energy resources, most of them under severe budgetary restrictions most of the time, to firing a boy up, lighting his fuse, or to inspiring him, through pep talks, pep rallies, modern career counseling, and drug rehabilitation seminars, to concentrate his immense energy resources on specific, realizable tasks. It is, however, one of the great misfortunes of civil society that, at the very moment at which a boy does learn to concentrate his energies or, in other words, to turn his energy into actual power, he usually suffers burnout, and then he tries to get his work done by throwing his weight around, delegating, cutting deals, cutting corners, and bringing in efficiency experts and energy conservation devices. If none of this works, a boy will try to fake it for another few years by fueling up on coffee and sweet rolls, by dating twenty-two-year-olds, and by hiding his essential powerlessness behind the wheel of an oversize gas-guzzling car and underneath Grecian Formula hair coloring.

How Boys Sleep and Keep Awake at the Same Time

When in an emergency or in a state of acute anxiety you occasionally have to call a boy at three-thirty in the morning and you apologize for awakening him, he will always tell you that it's all right, he wasn't asleep, he was just reading—and since the light is on, the television is on, and a copy of *TV Guide* is lying across his chest, he will half believe this himself. Boys believe that sleeping is a sign of weakness and moral slouch and, therefore, an activity better suited to girls than to themselves. They believe that, when a tense situation requires it, they can perform at peak levels, without any sleep at all, for days on end; and they also believe that when they do sleep, the impression they give of irreversible coma in fact only disguises heightened alertness to burglars and vengeful former girlfriends. Boys further believe that they do some of their most creative and lucid thinking while they're asleep, and this is why, when a boy is up against a really tough problem or an agonizing decision, he will usually want to sleep on it, or perhaps sleep it off, or at the very least take a nap.

What makes the pretensions of boys particularly ludicrous is that they not only sleep as much as anyone else, they have all but obliterated the conventional distinction between sleep and brain death. Despite what boys believe about their sleep habits, they in fact are capable of falling asleep anywhere, at any time, under any circumstances, without embarrassment, without apology, without changing their clothes, without brushing their teeth, and generally without any pressing need—often in the late morning, only an hour or two after they have gotten up. Moreover, when a boy announces that he is going to close his eyes for ten minutes, he will enlist bystanders to awaken him if he sleeps longer, he will nonetheless fail to respond to his name, threats, and repeated prodding, and he will eventually reawaken with no memory whatsoever of the fruit and cheese course or Labor Day weekend.

Boys and Loud Noises

Sometimes, when a boy is engaged in a perfectly normal discussion, say, of Soviet-American trade relations, he will suddenly and for no apparent reason insert an index finger into his mouth and dumbfound his dinner companions with the sound of a champagne bottle popping its cork; or he will stick a hand into his armpit and pump it in such a way as to counterfeit the splutter of a whoopee cushion; or he will do a moment or two of Howard Cosell or a Turkish rug merchant or a siren or surf. With whatever blunt instrument happens to be at hand—butter knife, pen, chopstick, swizzle stick, his own fingers, or a cattle prod—he will investigate the acoustical properties of wine glasses, water tumblers, rattan lounge chairs, aluminum siding, and his own and other people's heads. He will blow across the top of an empty beer bottle, turn up a radio, turn up the volume of the television set so that he can hear it over the radio, rev an engine, perhaps drive a sanitation truck through the sound barrier, crack ten knuckles, and belch—and only then, as if nothing at all remarkable had happened, will he return to his major point: that grain is one thing but high technology is something else and probably we shouldn't sell it even to our good friends the Canadians.

Boys in short are acoustical primitives and, as such, they are able to move back and forth between words and random, inchoate sound in a way that girls, with their easy and self-confident verbal expressiveness, find either amusing, mystifying, or mortifying, depending upon whether or not a particular girl is looking for a simple yes or no, whether or not the people on the other side of the table happen to be her parents, and whether or not a particular boy will at least have the good sense not to trot out his old fraternity party imitation of Richard Nixon's "I am not a crook" speech as delivered by Donald Duck under intense small arms fire in an Indy 500 pit stop.

What a girl doesn't understand is that not only the guitar serenading and the kettle drumming but most of the other aggressive ruckus a boy makes is in fact only sexual display, or strutting. A boy bleats and brays and rasps and toots "Dixie" on his car horn and makes obnoxious sucking noises in order to call attention to himself, and a girl ought to be flattered, even if she's not pleased. What perhaps ought to flatter a girl less is that occasionally a boy will rise to a fever pitch of noisiness and not think about her at all: Finding himself alone in a living room with a lethargic fox terrier, he will get down on all fours and, failing to produce the magic high-frequency whistle that he had hoped would drive the dog crazy, he will roll around on the floor, bark, howl, yelp, and yip, and in half a dozen other ways try to establish rapport with the dog in the dog's own language. On yet other occasions, half a dozen boys, only barely influenced by drink, will gather in an empty urban lot or perhaps on a street corner and, for half an hour at a time, until distracted by the distant wail of a fire engine, bay like sick coyotes at an eerie harvest moon.

Boys do not like, and do not respond to, subtle sounds. They are indifferent to wind chimes, jingle bells, onomatopoeia, any sound an English teacher would identify as tintinnabulation, and Oriental conundrums about one hand clapping. (If there is such a sound, boys would like to hear it; if not, tell it to the Marines.) Boys also have no use for silence except insofar as it is useful in covert operations. Inspired by the Westerns they watched as kids, they will, for example, frequently slip into a pair of moccasins and try to get some fun going by sneaking up behind a summer house guest and simultaneously letting out a blood-curdling war whoop and slamming her over the head with a day-old baguette.

Boys and the Testing of Limits

When a girl comes face to face for the first time with an unfamiliar animal, vegetable, or mineral, what she wants to know is: "What is its name?" "What does it do?" "Has it ever been married?" "Is it capable of sustaining intimate human relationships?" "Can it be taken to cocktail parties and weddings?" A boy in the same situation wants to know: "How far can I push it?" "How much will it take?" "What do I have to do before it will break, crash, disintegrate, wear out, call in the authorities, or refuse to see me anymore?" "What will it do if it's tortured?" Much to his regret, a boy spends most of his time, though, not on the Bonneville Salt Flats or at the Nevada weapons proving grounds but in bumper-to-bumper traffic on his local expressway or freeway. Consequently, a boy does not set land speed records or records for shortest pit stops. Rather he sets records for number of traffic lights missed, hours spent waiting for a transmission repair, flat tires, consecutive Saturday nights without a date, and accumulation of green slime in a bathroom sink. Occasionally, a boy will try to get out of his rut by going up against his own record in pushups, sit-ups, chin-ups, or laps in the neighbor's pool, and every once in a while, inspired by something he read in the *Guinness Book of World Records,* he will get it into his head to see how many onion bagels he can consume at a single brunch or how tall a tower he can make using only wine glasses and saucers. In polite society, much of a boy's legitimate desire to make a name for himself is understood, unfortunately, as "immature," "pathetically exhibitionistic," or simply "pathetic"—besides which, a boy himself will be suspicious of the chest pains and the tingling in his left arm, and he will consequently retire to the den to see if Dwight Gooden can set any new records against the Dodgers.

On the Competitiveness of Boys

When a boy is in his right mind, he will always take a mild irrational pleasure in locking horns with other boys, battling it out with other boys, getting a little sweaty and a little red in the face, and maybe even straining his muscles and knocking himself out. Even if a boy in his right mind invests immoderate energies in an absolutely meaningless game of darts, ping pong, or Clue, however, he will also be able to tell when he is engaged in a contest for something that really does matter—namely, power, status, prestige, a higher income-tax bracket, and showgirls—and then, however much lip service he pays to competition as the breeding ground of character and the guarantor of quality and reasonable pricing, his objective will simply be to get to the top of the pecking order as rapidly and as efficiently as possible, to grab up whatever scarce resources happen to be there, and finally to protect himself against new competitive challenges from below through restraint of trade, and if he has to gore a couple of people or stab them in the back while he rattles on about level playing fields, this is simply the price the system will have to pay for producing someone with insatiable ambition. A boy in his right mind will pick his fights carefully, he will walk away from the fights that he doesn't stand even an outside chance of winning, he will get even rather than get mad, and he will always make a special point of disparaging those competitive arenas in which he would sort of like to excel but, because when he was growing up his family didn't have a tennis court, he doesn't.

Unfortunately, a boy will sometimes not be in his right mind at all, and then he will either attach himself to glorious lost causes or, worse still, he will think that everyone really *is* talking to him and he will think that people really *do* want to make something of it, and he will go around opening doors and inviting strangers to step outside. When a boy is not in his right mind, his competitiveness, in short, will turn into a surly and aggressive combativeness; and then he will find himself engaged not in matches, and still less in games, but in aggravated conflicts and rivalries and, in the acute phase, either ugly confrontations that have to be broken up by uniformed police officers or arguments that don't end even after one party pulls out an atlas and demonstrates conclusively that Bolivia is in South America and not in Africa.

Some part of a boy, moreover, will always be out of his mind, and this is the part that bullies girls and tries to get them interested in thumb and arm wrestling championships and in ridiculous one-sided contests to determine who knows more about nuclear submarines; it is the part of a boy that is always telling a girl, "Hit me here, hit me as hard as you can"; and it is the part that spends the afternoon sulking when a girl not only does hit him hard but goes on to beat him soundly in miniature golf. Because most of the time a boy is totally unaware of how compulsively competitive he is, he will often be quite astonished, and in addition his feelings will be hurt, if a girl tells him to buzz off, or to take his aggression and his hostility elsewhere. Then he will not only remind her of what a great team player he is but he will provide specific dates and times as evidence of his helpfulness around the house and he will challenge her to name one person who is more cooperative and easier to get along with than he is.

Why Boys Think They Can Do It Without Any Practice

Although, when a boy approaches a podium, a playing field, a battlefield, or an audit, he will usually assure his well-wishers that he is pretty thoroughly prepared, that he has examined the situation from every possible angle, and that he is ready to meet any contingency, in fact he will usually not have prepared at all, he will have looked the situation over from exactly one angle, and he will not have even the vaguest idea what the contingencies are. A boy will indeed very nearly convince himself that adequate preparation is practically indistinguishable from overpreparation in that they both lead to the same overconfidence and complacency, and to a slowness to respond to surprises. He will further believe that adequate preparation and overpreparation are a lot more dangerous than underpreparation, and this is why, if he is given a choice, he will always take his chances not with the facts and the figures but with what he likes to think of as his fast and fancy footwork, his razzmatazz, his body English, and his smoke screens, his ability to talk his way out of just about anything and to tough his way out of whatever he can't talk his way out of, and his sister's term paper from the previous year. A boy will also figure that, in a really tight situation, he can always count on the other guy to be even less well prepared than he is. Paradoxically, when a boy has occasionally prepared religiously and even worked his ad libs to a high polish, he will assure his well-wishers that he is going to go in cold and wing it; then, if he carries the day, he's not just a hero, he's a natural, whereas if he blows it he can say, "I wasn't really trying"—unlike pathetic girls, who are always saying, "I can't understand why I failed, I worked so hard."

Boys and Spit

Boys feel an enormous self-confidence in the world because they know that when the faithful dog dies, when they've lost their Swiss Army knife, when the night sky clouds over and they can no longer steer by the constellations, when even a wing and a prayer fail them, they still have their own God-given native intelligence, and spit. Boys use spit as a cleansing agent, as a cosmetic (particularly for touching up their eyebrows), as a lubricant in sex, as a device for turning the pages of *Playboy,* as a means to making a hardball all but unstrikeable, as a solvent, as an adhesive, and as a weather vane. Boys also have a dim, but still untarnished, memory of the recreational uses of spit, and sometimes, when a boy is not in a tight situation at all, when it is not one or another of the industrial uses of spit that stands between him and certain death at the bottom of a tar pit, he will retire to the stern of a cabin cruiser, turn away from the wind, toss his head back, and see if he can still hawk anything like the twenty-seven feet that once, many years ago, won him fame in three separate school districts. The same boy, dressed up in town in a three-piece suit, can watch a derelict glom one down on the sidewalk, and not only will he outdo his date in outrage and indignation, he will throw in a perfectly gratuitous bad word or two about dust balls, sweat, and the current television season.

Boys As Fans

When a boy is temporarily distracted from his embarrassingly petty ongoing struggle to outmaneuver the assistant sales manager and, for an hour or so, he sits on the edge of his chair while superbly trained, larger-than-life-size athletes engage in epic battles for division leads and six-figure product endorsement contracts, he will, strangely enough, experience not his own smallness but his own bigness. At peak moments, he will actually be transported out of himself into a realm of joy, ecstasy, and pure rapture, or at the very least he will drag himself to the refrigerator for a beer and a sandwich. If his team somehow breaks out of the cellar and ultimately rides an unprecedented late-season winning streak to the top, he may even, for one magical moment, feel as if he could part seas and create light out of darkness—if they never break out of the cellar, he swears he's going to leave Cleveland for good. When a rational girl points out to a transported, or a crushed, boy that half of his heroes are in fact drug addicts and the other half are so scandalously overpaid that he ought to be against them on general principles, besides which the whole thing is only a game—what's he so worked up about?—a boy will concede that, yes, it is only a game, but he's not really in a very good mood, and even though he had been planning to go out and rent *Gone with the Wind* to reward her for being a good sport, it's now completely out of the question and, as for dinner, she's welcome to eat the rest of the saltines and then he'll be more than happy to call her a cab.

How Boys Get Into Trouble

The way boys see it, there's a lot more trouble out there than the average person realizes; the only problem is that the vast majority of it is dormant and, in order to get it going, you may have to toss pebbles at it, toss a lighted match at it, growl at it, stand it up on New Year's Eve, poke at it with a stick, make a couple of mock lunges at it, put your head in its mouth, or pretend to try to make off with its babies. Boys are not always good, though, at estimating just how much trouble there is in any one place, and this is why a boy will often get into real trouble only after he has decided to call it a day. He will, in other words, already have reassured himself of his strength, his derring-do, his crisis-management skills, and his knowledge of first aid. He will have had the thrill of disregarding a couple of verbal warnings and one or two warning shots. He will have had the excitement of passing up an opportunity to turn back, no questions asked, and another to be escorted out. He will even have enjoyed several extremely gratifying close calls and as many narrow escapes. A boy indeed may already be halfway home when suddenly he finds himself surrounded by four pieces of fire equipment, three squad cars, a minicam crew, maybe some girl's angry father, and an examining psychiatrist; and, at such a moment as this, he will usually have no tricks left in his bag other than to smile dim-wittedly and to trot out his old war-horse: "I wasn't doing anything, I was just standing around and the damn thing exploded."

When a boy finds more trouble than he bargained for and fast has to find a coat or a newspaper to put over his head, he is, strangely enough, never entirely miserable. The squad cars and the fire equipment and the flashbulbs and the handcuffs in fact give him the same cozy having-been-there-before feeling that other people in their adult lives get out of a nice bowl of homemade vegetable soup. A boy in really big trouble will generally try to get out of it by stonewalling, doctoring

43

books, burning tapes, reentering through Canada or Mexico, calling Mel Belli, pleading insanity, or sending flowers first thing in the morning. What a boy never quite grasps is that trouble is a highly regenerative mechanism and that it resembles a Chinese finger torture in that, the bruter the methods you use to get out of it, the deeper you get in. Later, when he tells the story at the office Christmas party, he nevertheless skims over the part about having to wire home for money, he changes the train conductor into three KGB agents, and just for the hell of it he throws in a ransom note, Mount Rushmore, and a nymphomaniac.

Twelve Common Warnings That Boys Take a Special Pride in Not Paying Any Attention to Whatsoever

"She's a man-eater."

"You can have a heart attack in five years, or you can cut down on the liquor, the cigarettes, the salt, and the red meat."

"Of course the game *looks* easy. Where do you think they got the money to build all those cathedrals?"

"Drive carefully."

"Just take it one step at a time."

ACHTUNG! PHOTOGRAPHIEREN VERBOTEN

"The lady has already told you that she did not meet you at a Jaycees picnic in South Bend, she did not meet you at the Cannes Film Festival in 1982, and she did not meet you at the Aga Khan's birthday party in Mykonos. The lady has no prior acquaintance with you whatsoever. Now beat it."

"That thing wasn't made to be stood on."

"Don't joke with those guys. They don't have a very good sense of humor."

"Be the bigger man."

"You'll never get it through Customs."

"Better take someone who knows the way."

Boys and the Dream of X-Ray Vision

If a boy were offered the choice of any conceivable super power, but only one of them, he would immediately eliminate flight, perpetual motion, perfect pitch, the ability to create something out of nothing, and good handwriting. He would in fact eliminate every last one of the super powers except for X-ray vision and invisibility and then in the final shakeout he'd be convinced he had to go with X-ray vision over invisibility on the theory that you could accomplish the same objectives with it but without having to move around so much and wear yourself out. The thing that has always astonished boys about the comic book hero Superman, with *his* amazing gift of X-ray vision, is that, instead of using it for the obvious purpose, namely, to look through the dresses and the sweaters and the skirts of Metropolis, he used it to foul up the plans of bank robbers. Boys harbor a mild secret contempt for girls, because while boys want to look through bedroom and bathroom and locker room walls, girls, they believe, only want to look through other people's files and closets and medicine cabinets and old love letters. For all the contempt that boys have for the girl failure of imagination, the best that X-ray vision has ever done for a boy in real life is win him an occasional root canal and indisputable evidence of a pre-arthritic condition in his neck. At some point in their lives, boys will look up at a fourth-floor plate-glass window and catch a glimpse of girls in colored leotards and tights and thick woolen socks bunched up around their calves, and they will feel a small stab of loss, not for the eternal impossibility of ever seeing through those leotards, exactly, but for the long time that they have not dreamed the dream of X-ray vision and for the unlikelihood of their ever dreaming it again.

Boys and *Playboy* and *Penthouse*

Though a boy would almost always sooner go to bed with a girl than with a magazine and frequently he will be so delighted with his dinner-table conversation that he will be convinced that he is going to go to bed with a girl rather than with a magazine, a boy will sooner or later be jolted back into reality. A girl, for example, may demonstrate her earnestness about getting to sleep early by bolting doors against him and, despite his begging from the pay phone on the corner, eventually take the phone off the hook; and then he will have no choice but to go to bed with a naked Congressman's wife, prime-time television stars, Ivy League brains, Southern Conference cheerleaders, or the occasional errant beauty contest winner, who, he learns in the paper the following morning, never intended to go to bed with him at all and now wants to apologize publicly to the many people who expected so much better of her. When a boy wakes up in the morning and finds the magazine by the side of the bed, *he* feels somewhat sullied by the experience, too. He cannot help noticing that the wonderful girls were just so much colored ink on glossy paper, and he feels himself to be a pathetic and contemptible creature with no hope of ever achieving lasting happiness. This feeling lasts until the next time he is at an airport newsstand and, drawn ostensibly by the no-holds-barred Mafia expose, the top-quality fiction, and the excellent stereo equipment guide, he plunks down a few dollars, thinks about asking out the cute hostess at the coffee shop at the Hyatt, and makes a mental note that, should he manage to strike out once again, he can always rendezvous later with Mimi and Darlene, amazing identical twins who, it says right here in black and white, like children and dogs and cozy evenings by the fire and lewd sex with anything that moves.

Boys and Girls in the Flesh

Drawing on personal experience, boys have come to a few simple and sustaining conclusions about sex. They have concluded that sex is the most important thing in the world and that, in any case, there *are* only two things in the world, namely, sex and everything else—besides which, ninety percent of everything else is either consciously or unconsciously a way of getting to sex. Boys have also come to the conclusion that there is some critical point—roughly as far away as the sun deck—beyond which, if they don't get some sex, they will go stark raving mad and have to be carried off in a straitjacket, and they have further concluded that girls, and in particular the slutty Madonna look-alike in 3C, are deliberately and sadistically committed to driving them to that point.

When a boy does get a girl to go to bed with him, he will always try to be gracious and ask her whether she would like a glass of brandy, a stuffed animal, dental floss, general anesthesia, a wake-up call; he will ask her if she would like the light on or the light off; and he will also ask if she has any serious objection to his handcuffing her to the radiator and running *Debbie Does Dallas* on the VCR. Because this is a first time and he is eager to make a good impression, he will kiss her on the mouth and he will even try to work up some enthusiasm for foreplay, and though he has big plans for the two of them to copulate at the earliest possible moment with her two best girlfriends, he will resolve to keep mum about it until they have established a bond of lasting intimacy and mutual trust, or at least until he has learned her last name. Although deep down boys aren't altogether certain that they aren't laughingstocks as lovers, on the surface, where they spend most of their time, they are quite smug about their technique, and they are fully convinced that it makes up for whatever they lack in honorable intentions, brute force, and endurance. A boy likes to think that his sexual appetite is enormous, but when he does find someone to sleep with on a regular basis and she doesn't just surrender, she moans, sighs, and begs for more, he tends to worry about when he's ever going to get his work done, let alone build his twenty-foot sailboat and coach a Little League team, and he also wonders why it is some people can't just enjoy "Nightline" and a good night's sleep.

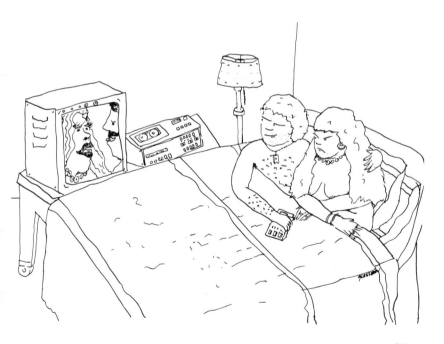

Fourteen Things That a Boy Always Says to a Girl on a First Date

"They're known for their hamburgers."

"If you're having the salmon, then we're supposed to have white wine, right?"

"I know you're going to think this is just a line, but you've got really amazing eyes."

"I'm talking too much."

"OK, let me try to explain it another way. When did the year one begin? January first, year one or January first, year zero zero? January first, year one, right? OK, so when does the twenty-first century begin? January first, 2000? No, because that's only 1,999 years after January one, year one. Get it now? The twenty-first century begins on January one, 2001. . . . What do you mean you don't *accept* that?"

"Picasso died? When did Picasso die?"

"Just give me a minute, and I'll *explain* why I voted for Reagan."

"Tell me something about yourself."

"Right, right, right."

"I'm not sure I understand exactly what you mean. You haven't spoken to your mother in five years?"

"I'll bet you're really good at your job, though."

"So how long were you married?"

"I don't know if you have to get up in the morning or anything, but if you'd like to come up, I make a really great tequila sunrise."

"So maybe another time."

The One Thing a Boy Always Says to a Girl on the Last Date

"I'll call you."

Why Boys Don't Call

Sometimes a boy goes out on what he thinks will be a routine Saturday evening date and he finds that his feet have left the ground and his head has lodged firmly in a big wispy cloud. His favorite dance music is playing on every elevator. Passing airplanes all seem to be headed for exotic destinations. The surf 'n' turf is grilled to perfection. The crystal sparkles. The waiters bow and scrape. The captain sends complimentary after-dinner drinks. Outside on the street, a cab appears out of nowhere, and the driver responds to his command with a snappy, "Yes, sir!" The scent of lilacs hangs on the night air. He can't tell if it's cloudy or bright. He has a strange, hard-to-express feeling that the streets look like a movie set. After a date like this, a boy may go for several consecutive days without thinking even once of the Danish simultaneous translator he found on a nude beach outside of Cap d'Antibes, and his biggest problem is to contain his enthusiasm and wait at least until morning to call for another date, since he doesn't want to scare her off.

Some weeks later, a boy will finally see the same girl on a second date, and she will turn out to be considerably shorter than he remembered her to be and not to have any depth of knowledge at all behind her assertion that Marciano could have licked Joe Louis with one hand tied behind his back. She will offer to lend him her copy of Laurie Colwin's *Family Happiness* because she knows he'll adore it. She will tell him that she really admires his resistance to mere trendiness but that he might also want to take a look at some of the more contemporary styles they have for men these days, and perhaps they could meet after work on Thursday and go shopping. She will also use the word "we" in two distinct sentences, and he will be pretty sure that in one of them he heard the phrase "shore in August." The pasta will be overcooked and he will splatter marinara sauce on his second-best tie. Rain will fall in thick slabs. A passing street tough will for no apparent reason call him an asshole. There will be no cabs. He will wonder what he ever saw in her in the first place.

This is why a boy doesn't call.

Or at least this is why a boy doesn't call until seven or eight years later when, all alone in a tavern late at night, he will suddenly remember precisely what he saw in her in the first place, he will locate her phone number in his address book, he will rush to the pay phone, and, despite the distinct background sounds of crying children and a gruff male voice asking, "Who's that?" he will have an impossibly hard time understanding why she can't drop everything and meet him in half an hour for a couple of Bloody Marys.

The Eight Principal Boy Lies

"No comprendo."

"Sure I'd like to talk."

"I love you very much."

"Fifty-three, fifty-four. Fifty-five at the most, officer."

"Jesus, I don't know. It was working fine when we pulled out of Salt Lake City."

"I think probably I'll just work tonight and turn in early."

"You're imagining things."

"I'm here, aren't I?"

Twelve False Statements, Not Exactly Lies, That Boys Actually Believe

"Girls really like me."

"I don't have moods."

"That's something I know a good deal about."

"Don't worry, I'll have it going for you in half an hour."

"You don't *have* to read the instructions."

"I was just about to call *you.*"

"Can do."

"A couple of nails right here ought to hold it."

"Hey, I'll pay you back first thing in the morning."

"Actually, I've been really busy lately."

"I can understand English."

"Talk to you soon."

What Actually Happens to a Boy When He Thinks He's Having a Feeling

Sometimes a boy gets carried away with himself and, thinking that he's not just having a feeling but a very powerful feeling, proposes marriage to people he's never seen in daylight or he writes phone numbers on cocktail napkins and leads perfectly innocent people to think that he is going to call. A boy who has gotten carried away with himself can cause considerable damage in the world—he can cause women to charge hundreds of dollars worth of resort clothes, let leases lapse, abjure their religions, and install call-forwarding—and therefore he should be given the widest possible berth. An exuberant boy promising marriage to a stranger should not be understood, however, to mean any harm. A boy sometimes simply enjoys his exhilaration, and he is equally happy to come down from it after a couple of hours, and, like a werewolf who has spent the predawn hours feasting on human flesh, he is always happy to wake up in his own bed, in his own clothes, and still have his wallet, his driver's license, and most of his money. Boys will in fact sincerely regret the havoc they cause and they would even be willing to pay modest reparations for any misunderstanding, if only they could remember exactly what it was they did, and if they didn't feel that the slight achy feeling wasn't already punishment enough. A boy is always a little surprised that a woman who has gotten in the path of his high-spirited cavorting does not share his sheepish pride and amusement and that sometimes, when he comes face to face with her at the coffee machine on Monday morning, she actually reproaches him. To the extent that a boy wonders what it was that came over him, he will usually attribute the whole awful mix-up to hunger, tiredness, or alcohol, or, if he is feeling particularly introspective, to his having been alone on an expense account in a strange town, or to his having caught a glimpse of himself in the mirror and really having liked the way his hair looked.

Why a Boy Frequently Has a Feeling Without Recognizing It As Such

Sometimes a boy will not merely think that he is in love, he actually will be in love, but instead of feeling his head swim and his pulse go faint, he will tell a girl that she'd be absolutely crazy not to accept the job offer on the other side of the country and he will be mildly annoyed if she orders the expensive appetizer. On other occasions a boy will be so angry that his face turns red and his eyes bulge, but not only will he insist that he's feeling fine, he will further insist that he has not raised his voice, he will calmly explain that shouting never accomplished anything, and he will concede only that he might be a bit irritated. Because a boy has spent so much time in the company of girls, he will know the names of a good many emotions, including jealousy, joy, grief, murderous rage, envy, loneliness, and vindictiveness, but, except when he is on a tear and temporarily out of his mind, he will personally experience all of them within the narrow limits between boredom and vague malaise. (Boys also tend to think of tiredness as an emotion.) The way a girl sees it, a boy either doesn't have any feelings or he has feelings that he is hopelessly out of touch with, and that's enough to make a girl cry. A boy believes that his impassivity, far from being a defect, is precisely what has seen him through his career confusion, his tax audit, his indictment, and numerous disappointing football seasons, and he also believes that, if he didn't appear to be mildly annoyed most of the time, sooner or later he'd be breaking down in public and people would stop saying how much he reminds them of John Mitchell and G. Gordon Liddy.

The Nine Principal Ethical Dilemmas of Boys

"How about if the spacecraft did have gun turrets on it but when the creatures got out they were carrying white flags?"

"OK, she's one game up on you, but you're still pretty sure that she's not going to last the set, and you really want to get her into bed afterwards. What do you do in this situation?"

"I really like her a lot. We have a great relationship. We've got the same taste in food, movies, everything. I really admire her, too. Her family's fantastic. Do you think I should tell her that I'm married?"

"If you were blind, do you suppose it would matter to you whether the woman you were with was beautiful or not?"

"The mailman puts your next-door neighbor's *Newsweek* into your mailbox by mistake. You spill coffee all over it. Do you put it under your neighbor's door as is, do you throw it out and forget about it, or do you put a new one under his door with a note?"

"Suppose you're living under some kind of fascist right-wing dictatorship, and they get you and your mother in front of this firing squad, and your mother at this point is really old and has a terminal illness, and they say that they're going to kill her unless you agree to have your legs and your arms cut off. So what do you do?"

"But what if the teller *doesn't* have to make up the mistake?"

"Does this look better with the collar in or with the collar out?"

"Suppose everybody thought the way you do, that superior people shouldn't be bound by the same petty rules that everyone else is bound by? Then what kind of world would this be to live in?"

Ten Questions That Boys Will Never Have the Right Answers to, No Matter How Hard They Try

"Where were you brought up? In a barn?"

"Do you want to poke someone's eye out?"

"Are you trying to get us all killed?"

"What do you think you're doing?"

"Where do you think you are?"

"Who do you think you are?"

"Who do you think you're fooling?"

"Do you remember how happy we used to be?"

"Are you sure we're going in the right direction?"

"Would you like to put your money where your mouth is?"

What Boys Really Think About Marriage

Although boys used to believe that marriage was invented by women, in the interest of women, so that they could play cards all day or just loll around in their housecoats, talk on the phone, eat candy, and generally freeload, boys have gradually come to understand that marriage was actually invented by men, in the interest of men, so that a hot meal would be on the table when they got home, so that they would never have to see ring around the collar except on television, and so that they could have as much sex as they wanted without having to go to the movies first or even brush their teeth. Boys further understand that marriage has been updated recently in order to make it less gloomy and oppressive for women, and they have nevertheless come to the conclusion that, even from their point of view, it is still a pretty good deal. Indeed, a boy really looks forward to getting into a marriage of his own someday, provided simply that the person he gets into it with has a job, her own American Express card, and rich parents, and provided also that she is in every way his superior, that she never asks him to acknowledge her superiority, even to himself, and, finally, that she makes him look good in public. When a boy does get married, he does so with someone whose superiority he is in fact profoundly skeptical of but who has nevertheless so thoroughly turned his head that when she licks his eyelids and says "God bless" after he sneezes, he can't tell whether it's incredibly endearing or it makes him sick.

What Boys Really Think About Relationships

When a boy tries to visualize his ideal relationship, he sees, first of all, a variety of state-of-the-art safety features, including numerous clearly marked emergency exits and sufficient round-the-clock lighting so that he knows where he is at all times and doesn't have to panic. Even if he and his partner lived together, had a child together, and shared the same toothbrush, the whole thing would be kept fundamentally casual, and "nice" in the sense of peaceful and non-dramatic; it would not necessarily be what a girl calls "good," meaning emotionally intense. He would not have to meet, be approved by, or indulge, anyone else's friends. He would be free to come and go as he pleased, even for months at a time, and he would have complete confidence that he would always be missed, he would always be welcome to pick up at the point at which he had left off, and he would not be reproached for not having called. He would be respected and admired; he would also be seen through, but not all the way. He would get precisely as much sex as he wanted, whenever he wanted it. In short, the whole thing would be entirely on his terms, and it would provide maximum pleasure and maximum ego gratification at minimum cost. Essential meaninglessness would not be held against it. Finally, the girl would at some point either insult him in front of his mother, deliberately wreck his stereo system, or borrow a hundred dollars and fail to return it so that, when he finally bolted, he wouldn't have to feel any guilt.

In the life that a boy actually lives, relationships have a variety of features that always put him on his guard or make him leap for a trench the moment a stranger of the other sex smiles at him in a friendly or encouraging way or asks him for directions to the Bureau of Motor Vehicles. Chief among these is a girl's conviction that a relationship must always be developing and growing and going someplace, preferably in the general direction of matrimony and with numerous stopovers in southern Europe, Hawaii, and the Caribbean along the way. A boy, meanwhile, would be perfectly content if it just stood around in one or two familiar places and occasionally ordered out Chinese or pizza. Under the best of circumstances, a girl will now and then want a boy to stand back from a relationship with her and admire it, cluck over it, and marvel at its strength and its progress. She will want him to remember how they met, what their song is, how he won her a pink stuffed unicorn by knocking over some milk bottles, and other uninteresting and humiliating incidents that he would just as soon forget. Also, she will expect him to do things with her.

A boy is terrified, moreover, that if a relationship should wake up in the morning and sneeze once or twice, she will very likely vivisect it. She will come up with a diagnosis: basically good but with a few things to work out, promising but conflicted, obsessive, weird sexually, neurotic, morbid, sadomasochistic, self-destructive, wait-and-see, transitional, limited, ill-advised, impossible, doomed, bad for both of us, I-can't-go-into-it-I'm-too-upset. While a girl is lunching on it with friends, poring over the horoscopes, and trying to get through to Dr. Ruth, a boy will try to blend into the woodwork; he will busy himself with the dinner dishes even though, strictly speaking, it isn't his turn; he will fall asleep. A girl, meanwhile, having diagnosed the relationship, will turn to the people in it. She will admit that she isn't perfect herself. Because of the way she was brought up, she probably feels things too deeply. As for him, he's insensitive. He doesn't feel his feelings. He doesn't feel her feelings. He's afraid to open up. He doesn't know how to give. He's not there for her when she needs him. He undermines her self-confidence and her morale. He talks with his mouth full. He never once brought her flowers. He doesn't really even want a relationship, what he wants is a sex-slave and a maid. A girl's good news is that there is nothing in the relationship that couldn't be fixed if the boy agreed to a massive personality change. A boy will explain that he likes his personality the way it is. Positions will harden, and paralysis will set in. In the worst of cases, a relationship will take on a life of its own, utterly independent of the two people who are in it, and it will have a tendency to go on and on and on, even if it is in a coma.

Given a boy's past experience and his inevitable dim conclusion that a girl's objectives in a relationship are different from his own, he will, as a rule, get into each new relationship only by accident. He will be enjoying what he thinks is simply a meaningless enough third or fourth dinner date. He will be looking forward to the sorbets and trying to think of a way to tell a girl that, though he has thoroughly enjoyed the past couple of weeks, he's not really looking for a relationship right now and he's too emotionally mixed up to have one anyway—and suddenly, much to his astonishment, he will see the point of no return slip past him on the starboard side and he will assure her that of course he would be delighted to spend Saturday with her painting her apartment.

Boys and the Lamaze Method

Despite his willingness to go along with Kegel exercises, abdominal breathing, effleurage, and shallow panting, a boy is never entirely convinced that there's anything even remotely natural about natural childbirth or that he couldn't just as easily reproduce himself by going crazy some Saturday afternoon with the office photocopier. When a boy has just spent the first trimester commuting to work with a box of saltines and sympathetic morning sickness, he asks himself: Will I ever be able to look at a female navel again without feeling queasy? Will I ever be able to look at a female again without feeling queasy? If this is what sex is really all about, how come modern civilization has spent so much money developing pills, foam, and Club Med, and why is it *Penthouse* never mentioned it in between letters from dominatrixes and love slaves? A boy finds himself thinking: What is this going to cost me over the long haul and, what with mobiles, collapsible strollers, and Mother's Day, how am I ever going to escape crib debt? Why me?

A boy nevertheless feels great pride and a substantially enhanced self-esteem when he participates, even incidentally, in the miracle of childbirth and more so when he begins to see some hope that if he just sticks with it, he may finally succeed in getting the little bastard to clutch up properly and stop hitting on the label side. A boy also feels great pride and enhanced self-esteem in the knowledge that if the mother of his child or, God willing, children should ever be called upon to assume high elective office, he will face up to his profound humiliation with as much dignity and aplomb as that guy John what's-his-name who was married to the woman who ran for vice president.

On the Memory of Boys

Though a boy may very well be able to name the entire pitching staff of the 1937 Brooklyn Dodgers and all fifty state capitals, not omitting Pierre and Bismarck, basically he thinks of the past as an arbitrary collection of events, any or all of which could as easily have gone one way as the other, and this is why a boy's story will always evolve in the telling and retelling and even his most humiliating disasters will sooner or later turn into dazzling triumphs. Because he is so casual about details, a boy will never understand a girl's indignation at his failure to remember the movie they saw on their first date, where he said he would take her for her birthday, the name of her grammar school, his manners, and his promise to call. A boy will have to be recklessly self-destructive to take the extremely controversial position that it is a matter of utter indifference whether the anniversary of the first time two people exchanged meaningful glances falls on a Wednesday or a Friday this year. But, in defense of his mental lapses, he will maintain that these details of personal life are rather like the incidents of history itself: The important thing is not that you remember the exact date on which the Battle of Gettysburg took place, the important thing is that you remember why it was such a momentous turning point in the Revolutionary War.

On the Vagueness of Boys

"Hi, this is Pam. I found your message on my answering machine."

"Oh, yeah, yeah, I called you."

"Well, how are you? I was just thinking about you."

"Well, I've been in and out a lot, and you know. Things."

"Sandy said she saw you at the Palladium wearing that bottle-green tuxedo jacket. She said you looked adorable."

"Really? I don't even remember being there."

"Jill said she saw you eating a Sno-cone in the park."

"Jill, yeah, that's that friend of yours with the hair—I don't know what you call it—and the sort of the waist, right?"

"Well, I'm really glad you called."

"I thought maybe we could do something, or something."

"Great. You mean . . . ?"

"Yeah, now, whenever."

"I'd love to."

"Do you want me to pick you up, or et cetera?"

"No, pick me up."

"OK, and I'll try to figure something out on the way over."

"Is there any particular way I should dress?"

"Well, you know, what you wear. Maybe we can do something this weekend, too, you know, all things being equal."

"Well, terrific. I'll be waiting for you downstairs."

"OK, sure, wait somewhere."

"Hi, Sandy, he just called and he's coming over to pick me up in half an hour. I think we're going to the French Shack for dinner, and then— I'm not quite sure of this, but he seems to want me to go up to his parents' summer cottage with him for the weekend; at least he was hinting pretty broadly."

Nineteen Things a Boy Will Always Say to a Girl in an Emotionally Charged-Up Situation

"You're overreacting as usual."

"If you'd just calm down a little, I'd be happy to explain."

"I am not shouting."

"I am not being unreasonable."

"You know who you sound like now? You sound exactly like your mother."

"All right, what's your point?"

"Where did you get that idea from?"

"Don't you understand simple English?"

"I wish you could see yourself on videotape."

"Now I'm going to tell you something that's really going to hurt you."

"Don't get hysterical."

"You're interrupting again."

"May I finish?"

"Didn't we have this same discussion yesterday?"

"End of discussion."

"Fini."

"I told you I didn't want to talk about it anymore."

"All right, you have the last word."

"Who? Me?"

Why, When a Boy Goes Out for a Pack of Cigarettes, There Is Always at Least Some Small Chance That He'll Never Come Back

Often when a boy has eaten every last morsel of his surprise birthday dinner, has professed to have liked it, and has also gone through such major motions as expressing appreciation for his new necktie, his spirit may not simply have stepped outside for a breath of fresh air, it may actually have taken up residence in another state, another country, or another century, perhaps with a Cree Indian girl and probably under an assumed name, and it may even have done so as long ago as junior high school when he first heard about sines and cosines and he worked to develop his aptitude for showing up and being absent at one and the same time. When a boy says he is going to get into the car and go down to the 7-Eleven for a pack of cigarettes or when, for whatever reason, he drops momentarily out of radio contact, he will, consequently, probably give some serious thought to going over one more horizon and seeing if he can't actually find his spirit, and some day he might almost do it, if only he thought that somebody else could be trusted not to botch up the Amalgamated account and if he didn't have to be at the dentist's first thing in the morning for root canal. Fortunately, a boy's body and a boy's spirit can withstand extended or even lifelong separation without serious side effects, provided he is indulged in his occasional grouchiness and provided also that he is humored a little when he occasionally gets it into his head that he is going to sell the co-op, sabotage the Amalgamated account, and live off of his poker winnings.

Why Boys Like, and Sometimes Need, to Swear

It is the abiding experience of boys that ordinary language lacks resources equal to the startling ideas, the bold opinions, and the strong, hostile feelings they have to communicate, and it is also their experience that in moments of crisis ordinary language fails them utterly. Boys, however, have one further incentive, expressiveness aside, for trying to sound like Eddie Murphy, or like a truck driver who has missed his exit. Boys remember with pleasure the magical power of obscenity to move total strangers to the opposite end of the bus and clear the balconies of movie theaters. Unfortunately for boys, though, obscenity has recently lost much of its stigma and, employed with sufficient virtuosity, it will even ensure the success of an HBO comedy special. "Asshole" has become almost a term of endearment, and "shit" won't get even a librarian to look up—besides which, the girls that a boy goes out with nowadays themselves frequently sound like drunken sailors on shore leave. Sometimes in a heated situation, a boy will try to recapture some of the former glamour of obscenity by calling a person, an institution, or an idea either bourgeois or lowlife. But this language will also seem pallid and lifeless, and he will eventually toss out a "fuck" or a "fuck it" in order to express his generally high level of frustration and as a kind of formal sign-off indicating that he is about to lapse back into his customary moody silence.

What Boys Really Think About Homosexuality

Ever since the locker room towel snap and other forms of harmless horseplay were rounded up for questioning, boys have been examining their consciences for symptoms and warning signs of homosexual tendencies, and they are pretty certain that they don't have any; moreover, they are often hard-pressed to discover in themselves even the vaguest sentiments of goodwill toward mankind in general or, for that matter, even toward their best friends. Boys, however, wish homosexuals no harm, though personally they never cared much for Truman Capote, and, under the usual hypothetical circumstances, they would even be willing to lay down their lives, et cetera. As much as anyone, boys are amused by the spectacle of leather and cruising and drag, and because they are so envious of the spell that homosexuals appear to cast over women, they will often try to cast some of that spell themselves by imitating homosexuals and schooling themselves in some rudimentary civilization. A boy, however, may learn what a pas de deux is and he may acquire a couple of bow ties, suspenders, and pleated pants, but he will still not succeed in casting any spell, because it will never cross his mind to love what she's done with her hair, he will never in a million years notice that she's feeling the tiniest bit existential, and it will certainly not occur to him that her paisley-painted shoes are absolutely fabulous, where did she get them? Indeed, the psychoanalysts should have realized from the start that, if locker room antics mildly suggested homosexuality, it is a boy's utter obliviousness to a woman that proves his heterosexuality conclusively.

On the Eating Habits of Boys

However much a wife, a mother, or a girlfriend may think that a boy can be pleased, or at least pacified, if she feeds him the one food that he always asks for three helpings of, boys are not really food sensualists, and they have very little confidence that food per se is ever going to contribute importantly to their stock of pleasure in the world. The object for boys, in fact, is not so much to taste, or savor, food as it is to fill up on it. Consequently, just as boys will always be inclined to think of themselves, deep down, not as human beings but as automobiles, cruise missiles, locomotives, or warships, they will always think of food primarily as fuel, as energy source, or as the stuff that keeps them going in the absence of decent cocaine or fear. This means that boys will frequently eat in anticipation of need, often only a few minutes after finishing dinner—they do this in order to avoid breaking down and experiencing hunger pangs in a hostile environment where the cook won't even understand the two simple words "over easy," let alone know that the gravy is supposed to be on the side and not touching the string beans. They will also frequently work up a huge appetite, allow the needle to drop below empty, and top off, wherever they are, on pizza, doughnuts, soup, hot turkey sandwiches, sides of French fries and cole slaw, and banana cream pie, not much caring how any of it is prepared. They will intercept food that other people are about to throw out or permit waiters to take back to the kitchen. They will tend to shovel and gulp. They will eat with their mouths open. They will also from time to time have to be hosed down after they've finished, and, though they have been socialized sufficiently to say, "Great dip" or "Terrific turbot," they will as often as not have no idea at all what they have eaten and, asked to recollect their meal only an hour or two after finishing it, they will typically say, "Huh?"

Though it is often thought that, in the absence of wives, girlfriends, mothers, and vending machines, boys would waste away and perish, boys are really quite resourceful about food. A boy will often prepare a perfectly respectable meal entirely on his own. Moreover, he will do so with considerable pride and flamboyance, and he will generally like to have a girl around to bear witness and testify, to clean up debris from the previous week's meals and snacks so that there's room to move around, to do the peeling, the chopping, and the grating, to roll up his sleeves and freshen his drink, and to step in and take over totally should he have to run down to the store for a newspaper or a lottery ticket. When a boy is really on his own, he will often promise himself that he will wash his dish, tuck a paper towel into his bathing trunks, and sit down and eat his dinner in front of *Entertainment Tonight* like a gentleman, but he will usually discover that, by the time he has turned off the burner, he has practically finished. Many people have the impression that boys are particularly mean before they eat; this may be so, but it doesn't explain why boys are also particularly mean after they eat.

Boys and the Dessert Cart

Sometimes a boy will sit through dinner in a first-class restaurant with nothing much on his mind other than the delight he expects to take in the marble cheese cake or the apricot soufflé. When the waiter comes to take the dessert order, the girl he has with him will casually order the three flavors of ice cream with hot fudge sauce, extra whipped cream, and cherries; and by the time the waiter turns his way, a boy will be so caught up in the monstrous logic of self-indulgence and self-denial that he will catch himself asking for only a cup of espresso. This impulsive behavior will fortunately, at very low cost, give him nearly the same thrill of self-forgetfulness for which he might otherwise have had to give up the last seat on a life raft, and his feelings of righteousness and revulsion will sustain him not merely through the sickening spectacle of her surrender to pleasure but for a good hour and a half afterwards. Later, when it has been established beyond a reasonable doubt that she is not going to spend the night at his place and he is not going to spend the night at her place either, he will drive a good half hour out of his way to a favorite all-night diner, he will order the piece of chocolate cake he had really wanted all along, and, after he has eaten it blindly and paid the check, he will absentmindedly pick up a couple of Mounds bars to chew on, on his way home.

Boys and Their Bosses

"You wanted to see me, Bill?"

"Yeah, uh, where was that thing?"

"The report I gave you?"

"Yeah, uh, well, no, actually, it was the . . . oh, shit, where did I put it?"

"The figures from Danny's territory?"

"Yeah, I had them."

"Maybe under that pile?"

"Yeah, uh, listen, maybe we ought to talk later on. Let me get this stuff together."

"Something wrong?"

"Well, just that I have to go upstairs later on to that goddamn budget committee meeting, and I wanted, you know, I wanted you to clear up . . ."

"The whole region?"

"I just don't want anyone poking holes in our numbers . . ."

"Don't worry. They've got steel girders on them. I had the new girl work the whole thing out before she went to lunch."

"I'm talking about that whatchamacallit, the whatzis."

"Should I close the door?"

"I'm telling you, the whozis."

"What the hell, it's all out of the book. If you want, I can touch a couple of bases. Maybe call up that idiot Smith over at Consolidated and see what they're going to do."

"Mmmm."

"Jan and the kids okay?"

"Oh, super. Well, actually, let me clarify that. Jan's all wrought up about this school thing. Of course, given the way . . . hold on, let me start that one over. Kids. You know. Hey, you see that goddamn thing in the paper this morning?"

"The Vikings game?"

"Well, that, sure. I mean, about how the Japanese come in in the morning and sing some kind of company song."

"So what you're getting at is..."

"I don't know, I was thinking of something more along the lines of ... you know, morale."

"Sensational idea."

"You think it's worth working something up on?"

"Stress the team aspect more."

"That's it."

"Pride."

"You've got it now. Run with it."

"Listen, Bill, when Walt leaves next week, can I have his office?"

"Can't that wait?"

"I'm not on shaky ground, am I? I already explained in that long memo why you can't blame me for the Houston fiasco."

When a boy comes out of a closed-door meeting with his boss and every secretary on the floor scrutinizes his face for signs of the weather, he will always be wearing his most enigmatic smile, but in fact he has absolutely no idea whether he ought to go out and buy himself a genuine leather briefcase and take his girlfriend for $150 worth of dinner in celebration of his imminent promotion or whether he should immediately remove from the office his Rolodex, a year's supply of letterhead stationery, and the files that prove that the company had full knowledge of the valve defect as a result of which it was necessary to evacuate three villages on the Tallahatchie river. For the next hour or so, a boy will try to remember what *Dress for Success* and *The Yuppie Handbook* say about short-sleeve shirts, he will shuffle the papers on his desk, and he will make repeated trips to the men's room. Later, when he has regained most of his powers of concentration, he will lose himself in a *Wall Street Journal* article about the coming shake-out in the fast-food pizza industry, and he will get to wondering if the answer doesn't lie in a cold beer and a medium-size pepperoni.

Eighteen All-Purpose Boy Expressions Without Which American Industry Would Shut Down Overnight

"Keep it short."

"I know the numbers look all wrong, I know legal says we're going to get in a tangle with Justice over it, I know p.r. says we'll have egg on our face in the newspaper, but my gut instinct says let's go with it anyway."

"You don't *have* to be smart. All you have to be is tough."

"Apples and oranges."

"The worst thing that's going to happen is you spend eighteen months in one of those country clubs like Allenwood."

"Look, it's not the firing squad. It's just a grand jury."

"The usual."

"So what do *you* think Iacocca would do?"

"All right, let me throw out a really whacky idea."

"Hey, what ever happened to old Charlie?"

"Profit and success and yachts and stuff like that are only part of it. There's also the thrill of seeing the other guy get creamed."

"Cover for me."

"Hey, listen, I told you. It was only an idea."

"No."

"Nah, Frannie's body, Jane's head, Mrs. Papadopulos's legs."

"You've got it all wrong. Roberta and Ted are just good friends. It's Norm in purchasing who's boffing her."

"Break it to him gently, make sure he understands it's nothing personal, and see to it that he has his personal stuff out of here by five o'clock with our best wishes, and if he ever needs a letter of recommendation or anything of that nature he'll always have our full support. I'll get in touch with security."

"Nice talking to you, too."

Nine Men Boys Really Have to Hand It to Because Not Only Did They Get Away with It but They Don't Even Appear Chastened

John Z. DeLorean

Claus Von Bülow

Frank Sinatra

Roman Polanski

Reggie Jackson

Richard Pryor

Richard Nixon

The General Dynamics Corporation

The General Electric Corporation

Nine Men Boys Really Feel Sorry for Because, Even Though They Seemed to Have the Other Guy by the Throat, They Failed to Cover Their Exposed Flank

Dr. Herman Tarnower

Lee Marvin

The 1981 Cincinnati Reds

General William Westmoreland

John Zaccaro

Harrison Williams

Jim Fixx

Bert Lance

Bert Parks

What Saturday Means to Boys

Saturday begins for a boy on Wednesday when he finally concedes to himself that the week is shot, the job at hand can't possibly be finished by Friday, and he might as well take it easy for the next few days and start in again on Monday morning, when he's fresh. Saturday peaks for a boy on Friday when he finds a parking space only two blocks away from his favorite Happy Hour, he spots a girl he thinks he can be happy with for the rest of his life, and he is quite convinced that he will walk three-quarters of the way down the bar and talk to her, too, if only he can decide whether he wants to pass himself off as a professional bounty hunter or as a Swedish businessman in town just for the weekend, and if he can keep himself from nodding off while he's deciding. A few minutes later, when the bouncer shakes him by the shoulders and tells him that he either has to wake up or get out, Saturday has already begun to develop serious respiratory problems, and it is in fact well on its way toward dying in its sleep even before the sun rises over the Road Runner and Bugs Bunny.

A boy will always be quite mystified and confused by his encounter with Saturday and, come Monday, he will wonder where it went, or if it ever even arrived. The reason for this is that a boy spends most of the rest of his week either going to, returning from, or seeking means to avoid some other person's drudge work, and therefore he tries to pack the whole of *his* affective and instinctual life, as well as his entire experience of freedom, into one lousy twenty-four-hour span that is barely elastic enough to furnish him with an extra couple of hours of uninterrupted sleep, let alone accommodate his needs to shave and not to shave, to clean the garage and not to clean the garage, to have a date and to keep his options open, and so forth. A boy sometimes thinks that he might just possibly beat the system by stretching Saturday into late Sunday afternoon or even into early Sunday evening—though then, of course, he would have to borrow from the time he has always earmarked for recovering from the weekend, whether he's had one or not, and dread. In fact, Saturday has been on an irreversible downhill course ever since, early in the week, he forgot the object lessons of his previous Saturday—the false promise of early morning sunshine, the inability of the muffler people to get him out in time for the kickoff, the utter bankruptcy of his options-open policy—and he began to get his hopes up. As a boy matures, it becomes clearer and clearer to him that he is unlikely ever to see a real Saturday except perhaps for a couple of hours on a holiday weekend or perhaps in the very remote future, after his retirement, when he's so inured to deprivation that he can't remember what it was he wanted of Saturday in the first place.

Why a Boy Acts Funny
When He's Sick

Whenever a boy gets a headache, a runny nose, a sore throat, or an unidentifiable pain in his side, his reason will take a powder and his imagination will go on a binge. He will convince himself that he has eluded early detection and is now in an advanced stage of brain cancer, tuberculosis, malaria, bronchial pneumonia, or syphilis. He will picture himself asking the doctor to tell it to him straight, and he will wrestle with the question of telling his first wife immediately, or just letting her find out that he's dead. He will resist any suggestion that he see a doctor, since it is not a doctor he needs, it's a priest, and he will also resist any suggestion that he get back into bed and take the day off. However much a boy is inclined to indulge and pamper himself when he is at the top of his form, he will indeed now drag himself off to his place of business, he will surround himself with antihistamines, throat lozenges, and Kleenex, he will blow his nose ostentatiously, and instead of closing the door after lunch, as he usually does, and dozing off, he will keep his door open wide and he will moan and groan in a shameless effort to elicit the sympathies of passers-by. As he had earlier resisted entreaties not to go to work, he will now resist entreaties to go home, and he will continue to resist entreaties to go home until, convinced that he has impressed everyone with his stoicism and his devotion to duty, he shuffles off at 2:30. He will spend most of the rest of the afternoon feeling vaguely annoyed with his mother for not having had a funny intuitive feeling that he was sick and for not having flown in from Akron to make cinammon toast for him, and he also feels vaguely annoyed with her because he knows that, when he does finally get around to mentioning to her that he has had a cold, she is going to make a big deal out of it.

When a boy has fully recovered, he will declare that his whole problem was simply overwork and exhaustion, and he will immediately call his travel agent and book two weeks in the sun. And when the girl he has taken along with him complains one morning that her stomach is a little upset, he will shake his head, he will sigh, he will ask if she minds if he goes snorkling for the day without her, and he will also go on at length about how it always amazes him that some people are susceptible to even the smallest changes in diet and temperature, whereas he can go anywhere, do anything, and somehow or other he never seems to get sick.

Boys and the First Amendment

When a boy sits down in a bar, or over a business lunch, and holds an audience of terrified subordinates spellbound by repeating, in his own words, whatever it was he read that morning in William Buckley's column, he thinks what a wonderful thing it is to live in a free country, and he resolves to exercise his freedoms still further by sitting down later and writing a scathing letter to the local newspaper in response to a recent editorial on the need for additional trash containers at the county zoo. Unfortunately, a boy spends less time than he would like in the marketplace of ideas and more time than he would like in tangled interpersonal relationships where most of what he wants to say is unacceptable not because it is dangerously heterodox but because it is mean, impolite, obscene, or ungrammatical. When a boy has managed to restrain himself temporarily and then, finally, driven beyond endurance, insists on exercising his First Amendment guarantees and says, "You make me sick," he always, for one wonderful moment, feels completely unburdened and free of malice. Then he feels intensely guilty. Then he wishes he could unsay it. Then he has to get down on his knees and swear he was only joking, just as if he lived in Poland or Cuba.

Boys and the Fifth Amendment

A boy feels indebted to the First Amendment for giving him the right to lecture total strangers in piano bars on the strengths and weaknesses of the Strategic Defense Initiative, even when those strangers wish he would shut the hell up. He feels indebted to the Fifth Amendment for giving him the right to shut the hell up when other people want to know where he has been until such an ungodly hour, what he has been doing there, for how long, why, and with whom. Unfortunately, a boy can only wish that other people valued his rights as much as he does and that, every once in a while when he gets home a little late, already tired and probably a little drunk, he didn't have to be made to feel as if he had just stumbled into the political section at police headquarters in some Third World backwater and then have to stay up half the night while somebody asks him the same boring questions over and over again, won't be tricked into changing the subject, won't take a polite lie for an answer, won't be bought off with the promise of a weekend in a country inn, and keeps turning off the television set. The sad truth is that if a boy prefers not to cleanse his conscience with a full confession, it's not that the truth is so incredibly incriminating but rather that he would be profoundly embarrassed to have anyone else know how little he has actually been doing, how little real pleasure he has gotten from it, and how incredibly much it cost.

What a Boy Thinks About When He's Not Thinking About Anything

Mil, novecientos noventa y nueve, novecientos noventa y ocho, novecientos noventa y siete, novecientos noventa y seis, novecientos noventa y cinco, novecientos noventa y cuatro...

This room, this house, this block, this street, this neighborhood, this city, this state, the whole country, the Western Hemisphere, the world, the solar system, the Milky Way, the universe, the cosmos...

A-a-a-a-and starrrrrring...

...for sacred skies, for lah-lah waves of grain...

Mary, hi, how ya' doin'...No...Hello, Mary, this is...No...So, what's going on...Yours truly, here...Hello, Mary, you don't know me but...Hi, Mary, guess who!...Hiya, gorgeous, miss me?...What do you mean, who is this?...

Felice, Barbra, Lonnie, Janet Borg, Janet Bluestone, Judy, Judith, Ann, Angela, Annette, Cathy, Catherine Costello, Beatrice, Debbie Deane, Elinor, Elaine, Louise, Lou Ellen, Jill in Atlanta, Patti, Nan, the two Karens, oh, and Cheryl...although not technically...

MILWAUKEE MILK WALK KEEL MEEK MEAL LIME WAKE WEEK MILE MAIL MALE KALE LIKE MAKE WAIL MAUL LAKE LAME WILE WEAK

$42,857 \times .1125 \div 12$

Yaz in left field, Mays in center field, the Babe in right field; let's see, Koufax or Feller on the mound, Aparicio at shortstop, Gehrig at first, maybe Joe Morgan at second, Brooks Robinson at third, Berra behind the plate and the Goose in the bullpen and the Japs can put up anyone they fucking well please.

Eric, Jonathan and Philip and what we do is, we rent the candy store *next door,* and we run it for a month or two as if it were a real business, and all the while we're tunneling, tunneling, tunneling. We've got about a thousand sticks of dynamite, and we've got Billy waiting at the airport with a Cessna 180 and the passports. Then we unload the story on Paramount for another million.

Boys and the Dream of Untold Riches

If a boy had all the money in the world, he would probably live more or less the same way he lives right now, with a couple of minor differences: he would do it out of a quality downtown hotel with efficient round-the-clock room service and a switchboard that still knows how to take a message; he would hire lawyers to figure out a legal way for him to keep a harem and to prevent the girls from scrapping with each other and making unreasonable demands on him; he would employ a public relations firm to ensure that he got the proper high place on the Forbes 400 and also to deny that he had any money at all so that he wouldn't have to deal with too many paternity suits or be bothered by opportunistic second cousins; he would employ an intelligence service to track down and humiliate every last person who had ever doubted him, cheated him, welshed on him, insulted him, or underestimated him. Because a boy is a nice guy, he would also buy his mother a palace with lots of servants, a swimming pool, ornamental fountains, and topiary; and, because he believes in the responsibility of the very wealthy to contribute to basic research in the social sciences, he would give away large sums of money himself to see whether other people would use it wisely or if it would corrupt them. He would set aside one other large sum for experiments in making people jump.

Boys are pretty sure, however, that they are not going to put their hands on untold riches simply by following their current career paths, and this is why they spend so much time checking the coin returns in public phone booths and going to the race track, and it is also why they make their girlfriends swear on their lives not to try to rip off their ideas for restaurants and screenplays. While a boy is waiting for untold riches to descend upon him, he makes do and keeps himself in form by comparison shopping at the annual yacht show and overtipping hat-check girls.

Boys and Pocket Money

Boys have not been able to help noticing that, as the number of credit cards they carry has increased, the need they have for folding money has diminished, and they would perhaps not see folding money at all if they did not occasionally take a date to dinner at the best restaurant in town and if cash were not the form in which they preferred to have the date reimburse them for her half. When, for whatever reason, a boy has recently had a wad of twenties or fifties in his pocket, he will be quite bewildered as to where it all went, and he may in fact not remember anything other than that he had a haircut, picked up some dry cleaning, bought drinks for a couple of people he didn't know, and contributed a dollar and change toward the receptionist's birthday party. It has not escaped boys that money is doing a lot less talking than it used to and that, at car rental agencies and airline ticket counters, it can barely get out a coherent syllable. Like most modern people, boys like to think of themselves as sophisticated money managers, and this is why they tend to keep their liquid funds not in their pockets and not under their mattresses but in interest-bearing checking accounts so that they can take advantage of the float and from time to time increase their net worth by two cents here, four cents there.

Boys and Their Pockets

Unlike girls, who usually tote their belongings in a single, crippling, over-the-shoulder sack, boys spread out their necessaries through a decentralized system of containers, known as pockets, and consequently they feel superior to girls for what they believe to be their more finely honed survival skills, their invulnerability to purse snatchers, their free hands, and not least of all their ability to make it through the day without lip gloss or cuticle softener. On any particular day, a boy might go about his business with ten or a dozen of these pockets. He will use the higher ones as a desk and safe deposit box for unmailed rent checks, newspaper clippings, an address book, documents too dangerous and too incriminating to leave lying around the house, and a list of the same ten goals he's had since 1981 (none crossed out); he will use the lower ones as a piggybank-toolbox-trash can for loose change, keys, nail clippers, and breath fresheners, for the lucky silver dollar without which he believes he would never have lived to tell about his shrewd business dealings in a Bogotá alleyway, for used Kleenex to ripen in, for the candy wrappers and cherry pits which, in a spirit of good citizenship, he decided to hold on to until he came to a proper receptacle, then reconsidered and concluded he might as well hold on to for a while longer, and for the warehousing of lint, string, sand, rubber bands, sagebrush, tumbleweed, and cactus. A boy may also go about his daily business with such auxiliary non-pocket pockets as the glove compartment of a car, the trunk of a car, the back seat of a car, an attaché case, a duffel bag, maybe a U-Haul, and maybe an already overburdened girl who doesn't have the killer instinct to say simply, "No, thanks," when he asks her, "Do you think you could fit this blowtorch into your purse?"

Boys in fact are so pleased with themselves for not having to lug lip gloss, so convinced that they carry no baggage at all, that when they lose something important and they go to look for it in the only place it

could possibly be, namely, among the banana peels and coffee grounds in the kitchen garbage, they need to have a woman around to ask, "Have you checked your pockets? Have you checked the pockets of the trousers you wore yesterday?" Boys also need women to remind them to check and empty their pockets before their clothes go for a washing, and it is the stout and unshakeable conviction of boys that they have already done so that accounts for both the large number of faded dollar bills in circulation and the remarkable volume of Kleenex lint in apartment building washing machines.

When boys run out of other subject matter late at night, they can always get a good conversation going about which is the best pocket for carrying a billfold or a wallet, if you want to frustrate pickpockets. Some boys argue vehemently for an inside suit jacket pocket and others, with equal vehemence, for a front trouser pocket. Boys who carry their wallets in their back trouser pockets make no case that it is safe exactly but only that they have lightning reflexes and, at the merest touch, their hair trigger is going to go off, and the poor unwitting son of a bitch is going to have to be scraped off the sidewalk.

How Boys Go Out of Style

When a boy steps through his front door in the morning, full of vim and ready to take the world by the neck and throttle it, it will never for a moment cross his mind that the people passing him on the street mistake him for a head waiter, a shoe salesman, a Salvation Army officer, a math student, a pool hustler, or a mugger. Indeed, a boy will not suspect that there is anything fundamentally wrong even if the deli guy snickers and the receptionist looks up in horror and his boss's secretary gasps. A boy will always believe that he has carved out for himself a strong personal style, however subtle and however unnoticeable to the naked eye, and he will always be very sensitive about this style, and when he is made to feel self-conscious he will automatically check to make sure that his fly is closed and that his tie is still tucked neatly and smartly into his pants. A boy's confidence in himself notwithstanding, what the way he looks really reflects is his intense anxiety and confusion about fitting in, standing out, what standing out and fitting in have to do with getting ahead, his relation to authority, his relation to his mother, his relation to women in general, his last trip outside the continental United States, aging, and every movie he has ever seen with James Dean, Fred Astaire, Harrison Ford, or the latest punky or preppy adolescent upstart, and *Miami Vice*.

When from time to time a boy dimly perceives that, in his own environment, not only are the guys in the mailroom dressed in a way that he doesn't understand but so are the comptroller and two vice presidents, his anxiety and his confusion will take off into the stratosphere. He will suddenly become aware that he is the last guy in the bar car with muttonchop sideburns and lapels out to his armpits, and he will finally understand why he never gets a decent table even in the company cafeteria. A boy awakening from a deep fashion sleep will rush to the nearest men's department, he will snap up a dark green sharkskin suit so incredibly raffish that its price was slashed twice before it was even put out on the racks, he will also snap up an Indiana Jones hat and a safari jacket just to be on the safe side, and, over dinner that evening, he will ask his girlfriend if she doesn't think that that rounded collar she's wearing is a little passé, and has she ever considered more of a padded-shoulder look?

Why Boys Can't Stand to Shop

When a boy occasionally finds himself on an up escalator between two high floors of a major downtown department store, he will sometimes freeze up completely, and he will as often as not experience vertigo, shortness of breath, and nausea, and then he will panic and have to fight hard not to reverse direction and hack and push his way through innocent and harmless women shoppers in order to get back out to the street as quickly as possible; moreover, he will wonder what ever lured him into this particular region of hell in the first place. A boy will have this acute panic reaction when it occurs to him that they might actually have what he was looking for, that he will have to wait and perhaps even stand in line in order to get it, that at some point he will probably have to take off his pants, and that when he does take off his pants he won't know where to put his wallet—besides which, if he wanted as much contact with a stranger as he is now all but certain to have with a salesperson, he'd get married. A boy can also not help suspecting that, faced with such a wondrous array of styles, colors, and shapes, he is bound to make a mistake; and, furthermore, he's gotten by this long without a dress shirt, he can certainly go another week. When a panicking boy is in the revolving door and almost in contact with fresh air again, he will as often as not see a wondrous girl on her way in, he will make a complete circle without ever once really touching the street, and he will follow her all the way to the cosmetics counter where, from a respectful distance, he will watch her purchase a complete skin care program with no trouble at all, and he will figure that, as long as he's already in the store, he might as well make a pass through lingerie.

Why a Boy Believes Himself to Be Immune to Advertising

A boy believes that a sucker is born every minute and that this is why a girl will stock her clothes closet, her refrigerator, and her bathroom with name-brand soft drinks, shoes, blue jeans, cosmetics, and shampoos, all of which, if they were any good in the first place, wouldn't even *have* to advertise; and it is also why, when he decides to try his own hand at advertising and he takes out three or four lines in the personals, he figures he might as well describe himself as intelligent, good-looking, financially secure, and sensitive. A boy believes that he, meanwhile, unlike other people, can take repeated exposure to the most corrupt Madison Avenue hype; he can hum the jingles; he can toss around the slogans in his conversation; and, thanks to his innate skepticism and his high resistance to psychological manipulation and emotional pleading, he will be alert to subliminal messages in feature films, he will buy Right Guard on its merits, and he will always ask for Savarin coffee by name because, in his heart of hearts, he knows that El Exigente isn't nearly as demanding as he is.

Boys and Beer Cans

A boy experiences quite enough traumatic, heartbreaking loss in his life—the death of the pet turtles, of a fox terrier or two, of numerous pairs of blue jeans and sneakers, of the '73 Mustang he left attached to a telephone pole—without also having to give up every last beer can he lays hands on, just because he happens to have emptied it. If a boy does not outright collect or hoard beer cans, he may from time to time in his life press one or more of them into service as ashtrays, pencil holders, soap dishes, party hats, bookcase risers, or intercoms, and he will also occasionally stockpile the pop tops in the hope that he can interest some girl in weaving them together into a necklace or a sweater vest. A boy, moreover, even at his most unsentimental, will never merely throw a beer can out—he will crush it in a display of hand and forearm strength, place it on a city street for the pleasure of the sound it makes when it is run over by a car, set it on a mailbox down by the rural route and shoot BBs at it from twenty feet, or, despite his occasional flirtation with conservationism, lob it out of a car window at sixty miles an hour as an expression of his contempt for the way the Interior Department housekeeps the National Parks. A boy, paradoxically, has no comparable attachment to the empty Coke can, which he is willing to divest himself of with no ceremony at all or even return for the five cent deposit, or, for that matter, to the Jack Daniel's bottle, which, once he's given someone a loving pat on the head with it, he is willing to consign forever to the oblivion under the front seat of his car.

Boys and Beer

Even if a boy has learned to order Chivas or Rémy or Perrier in public, he will always have a sentimental attachment to beer for the simple reason that it was the very first substance he ever learned to abuse and also because, taken in sufficiently large quantities, it breaks up the monotony of operating heavy machinery and long-distance car travel. A boy regrets that, whereas in the old days beer inspired him to some of his more imaginative acts of vandalism and some deeply sincere, however ill-advised, predawn phone calls to his favorite English teachers, nowadays it primarily makes him drowsy, it makes him try to prove how much he can still recite by heart from Joyce Kilmer's "Trees," and it makes strangers on the street wonder why it is that he carries a basketball under his shirt.

Boys and Aliens in General

A boy can never be entirely certain whether any particular alien is going to turn out to be powerful and menacing; grubby, arty, and subversive; or tired, disoriented, and homesick—and this is why he will generally have such a hard time deciding whether to set an ambush for it and bash its brains out, put it under twenty-four-hour surveillance, or charge it $350 for a ride from the airport to a midtown hotel and all the while watch if for quirks and fractured idioms so that he can work up a devastating impression. On rare occasions, a boy will find himself infatuated with an alien—say, a girl with purple hair or a guy with a big idea. Then he will set up a little household with his alien, he will explore the mysteries of slam dancing, class struggle, or deconstruction, and he will either try to convert other people to his exotic new way of life or, convinced that he is having an experience as rich, magical, and ineffable as if he had come face to face with something weird in a Steven Spielberg movie, he will keep to himself even more than usual. On other rare occasions, a boy will feel not merely alienated but alien, and then he will put on a dress and heels, he will try to persuade the other customers in the doughnut shop that he is Jesus Christ or the President of the United States, or he will attempt an unfriendly takeover of CBS.

Boys and the Japanese in Particular

Until recently, it had never crossed a boy's mind that his patriotism was going to be put to the test every time he went out to buy a new car or a new stereo system or even a lousy digital watch or a hand-held calculator. Indeed, if anything is cutting into a boy's sleep, and even cutting into his late morning nap, it is the terrible gnawing feeling that low-cost foreign labor and unfair non-tariff trade barriers are pushing him, and everyone he has ever known and loved, right to the brink of ruin. A boy does not believe that America can survive simply as a service economy specializing in throwing good money after bad to criminally overmortgaged make-hay-while-the-sun-shines Latin American debtor nations; and he does not believe that, in the home market, it makes very good sense to give up steel, heavy machinery, and the garment industry in favor of chocolate chip cookie boutiques and suntan parlors. A boy, moreover, has very little confidence that Lee Iacocca, however heroic that great man's energies, can hold the line against Japan, Inc. singlehandedly, and this is why, whenever he has left yet another car in a ditch on the side of the road, he will be sorely tempted to take out a bank loan for an additional $10,000, bypass the Honda and the Datsun dealerships, and get himself a BMW, a Porsche, or a Mercedes.

Boys and Their Friends

Because friendship, for boys, has everything to do with intensity of feeling and nothing at all to do with frequency of contact, a boy is always capable of persuading himself that his three best friends are the college fraternity brother, now living three thousand miles away on the other coast, with whom, except for the exchange of annual corporate Christmas cards, he has had no contact at all since 1978; the half-crazed illegal-alien house painter with whom once, in a Greyhound bus station, he had an amazing all-night conversation in which religion, sex, and politics all, for one dazzling moment, assumed their proper places in a rational and well-ordered universe—this person, for all practical purposes, having disappeared off the face of the earth; and the incredibly gifted high school pole-vault star and future orthopedic surgeon who, as a result of a freak late-summer electrical storm, has actually been dead for most of the past decade. A boy at any given moment may also feel particularly close to two or three living and dead dogs, and he will count as his "very good friends" and "close personal friends" a handful of medium-range celebrities to whom he has confided, in embarrassed moments on the receiving lines of corporate awards dinners, "It's a real honor to meet you, I've been admiring your work for years, and I think the new weather map is a major improvement."

Boys are sufficiently on to themselves, however, to know that these highly idealized, or imaginary, friendships have virtually nothing to do with reality and that, in fact, they don't have any friends and, moreover, wouldn't know what to do with one if they did. Boys also know that for the day-to-day purposes of trying out jokes, borrowing a ten, moving furniture, winning at squash, making deliveries in no-standing zones, and nauseating and horrifying girls, they can get on quite nicely with a collection of obnoxious and unpresentable lowlifes they think of as pals, chums, partners in crime, cronies, and buddies.

Boys and Their Buddies

Though a boy's buddies believe that it is they alone who are responsible for his pulling back from ill-fated wedding engagements and harebrained oil and natural gas deals, a boy will always privately think of his buddies as sidekicks, seconds, right-hand men, disciples, harmony, or potential bail, or as comic relief if he thinks of himself as a latter-day Immanuel Kant, or as straight men if he thinks of himself as The Three Stooges. A boy's buddies always have names like Big Al, Big Wally, Schnoz, The Man, My Main Man, J.D., or Abercrombie, except when they are being introduced to girls and they turn into James Abercrombie III, "who is famous for setting fire to a dead chicken and throwing it through the ground-floor window of the Scarsdale police department," or, if the girls appear to be in need of a good liberal arts education, "my associate Dr. Watson," "my associate Dr. Caligari," or Johnny Walker, Jim Beam, Ernie Banks, William Proxmire, or Merrill Lynch. Boys are chastised a lot for chumming and buddying around without ever expressing their feelings to one another. This charge is unfounded. Boys express their feelings to one another constantly. Their feelings are:

"The Knicks suck."

"Goddam straight those universities ought to get their endowment money out of South Africa."

"You asshole, you let her walk all over you."

Eighteen Things Every Boy's Best Friend Tells Him

"Thick and thin, right? Blood brothers, right?"

"She's too good for you."

"Let's synchronize watches."

"The blond one's mine. I saw her first."

"I'll bet if you hit him in the stomach, though, he'd go right over."

"OK, so a minister, a priest, and a rabbi are up in this airplane, and all of a sudden the pilot says they're about two hundred pounds heavy, so . . . you've heard this."

"What I'd do if I were you? I'd sue 'em."

"You have to get to know her."

"If she asks, I was with you."

"Women."

"I'll tell you what the problem is. No speed, lousy defense."

"Five points if you hit the nun."

"I thought you were supposed to be my friend."

"I'm for keeping going. That way we make Key West by sunup."

"Then we just walk out, right through the front door, cool as kings."

"Compared to what?"

"As usual, you don't know what you're talking about."

"Rotsa ruck."

Why a Boy Never Runs Out of Socks

When a boy is getting dressed in the morning and, much to his astonishment, he discovers that he is not already wearing socks from the night before, he will always go first to his underwear drawer and he will immediately be reminded that it is weeks since he found anything there other than the single argyle he has been holding on to in the hope that someday its partner will turn up under the bed, the white sweat sock in which he keeps an emergency ten dollars, and the tie clasp his mother gave him for Christmas, still in its original gift wrapping. When a boy follows the trail of soiled underwear from the bedroom into the bathroom, by contrast, he will always find two socks that nearly match on the floor next to the hamper. A boy will sniff these socks and he will hold them up to the light, and not only will he be convinced that he can get another three or four days out of them, he will wonder what ever gave him the idea that there was anything wrong with them in the first place.

Why Boys Like to Fix Things

When an otherwise perfectly good household object breaks beyond repair in a girl's hands, her first instinct is to go at it with her most sophisticated cleaning products in the hope that they will get it going; then, if cleaning doesn't work, she kicks it or bangs it a couple of times; and, if that doesn't work, she calls in the Salvation Army to haul it off for the benefit of poor people. When an otherwise perfectly good household object breaks beyond repair in a boy's hands, he throws it straightway into the trash and he keeps it there indefinitely while he decides whether he wants to tinker with it from time to time or actually throw it out. Because a boy owns so many inoperative typewriters, defunct television sets, and sluggish air conditioners that do *not* fit comfortably in the trash, and because he also lives amidst dripping faucets, noisy radiators, and badly caulked windows, a girl will frequently forget her tenuous status as a guest and tell him that he inhabits a dump, and she will also occasionally get into really big trouble by throwing out, as patently useless, something that he was planning to get at with pliers, Rustoleum, and a couple of rubber bands first thing on Saturday morning. A boy likes to try his hand at fixing things for a number of reasons, but chief among them are the challenge of the sticker that says NO USER-SERVICEABLE PARTS INSIDE and, second, the gall he feels that a refrigerator repairman should drive a later-model car than he does.

When a boy has pooh-poohed all entreaties and aimed his basketball at a girl's fireplace and broken the heirloom plate on the mantelpiece, he will always chide her for not having kept it in a safe place, he will tell her not to worry, and later, when he has laboriously pieced it together with Krazy Glue and pronounced it good as new and she bursts into tears, he will promise to go to her high school reunion with her after all and he will also show her how admirably the plate will serve as a Brillo pad holder under her kitchen sink.

Why Boys Like to Total Things

Boys believe that a factory-fresh automobile, particularly if it has been meticulously detailed by Italian master craftsmen for a base sticker price in excess of $30,000, is one of the great achievements of human civilization; and this is why boys are never certain whether they want to break in such a car slowly, hold it to the legal speed limit of fifty-five miles an hour, and have it hand-washed every week or if they wouldn't just as soon gun it immediately to the eighty or eighty-five mile per hour cruising speed that it was built for, aim for the nearest tree or telephone pole, and get the suspense and the waiting over with. A boy who has recently totaled something nice—a car, a small plane, or a perfect marriage—will lie low for several weeks. He will obey all the laws and ordinances. He will turn in early. He will avoid bad influences. He will do all of this until he has been kept late at the office some stormy evening and, on his way home, he sees the gate at the railroad crossing just beginning to go down and he is convinced that, if he just hits the accelerator hard and scoots around the Toyota and the Chevy, he stands a pretty fair chance of making it.

Why Boys Like to Break Things

The way boys see it, much of the paraphernalia of the world they live in was actually meant to be broken, and this is particularly true of records, rank, rules, the sound barrier, new ground, promises, and dates. Boys also believe that most of the so-called consumer durables they fool around with are, for all practical purposes, broken by the time they come off the factory floor, and these things don't really even have to be broken; they will usually simply fall apart if they are run for a couple of minutes on high. Though, in the absence of alternatives, a boy will almost always be happy to wreck something for which he personally paid good money, he will also take a great deal of pleasure in breaking things that belong to someone else, and this is why he will so often welcome an opportunity to saturation-bomb somebody else's northern provinces or to attend a stag party or a Shriners convention.

Seven Scientific Experiments That a Boy Believes Would Answer Most of the Questions That Are Still Bothering Him About the Way the Physical Universe Really Operates

Find a tooth somewhere, human or animal, and leave it overnight in a glass of Coca-Cola Classic. Find out once and for all whether it does dissolve or it doesn't dissolve.

Lace a cat's regular afternoon beer with LSD. See what happens.

Have a child with the smartest woman you can find, regardless of what she looks like. Keep the child out of the hands of the mindless, sub-mediocre educational establishment and the idiot clergy. Start it on chess and computer science even before it can talk. Drill it in mathematics and the physical sciences for ten or twelve hours a day and also make sure it gets plenty of exercise. Play Russian-, Chinese-, Arabic-, and Spanish-language tapes while it's sleeping. See if it isn't possible to shape a human being who's completely open-minded, completely rational, and completely liberal.

Try the same experiment on a girl child. See if it can't be shown that there's nothing basically wrong with girls, either, and that they could be completely open-minded, completely rational, and completely liberal, too, if only they could be kept away from *Vogue, Lifestyles of the Rich and Famous,* and psychotherapists and astrologers.

See if the office computer can't be programmed somehow so that Citibank deposits $300 a week in your checking account, tax-free, no questions asked.

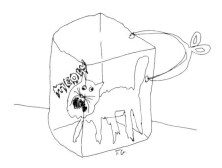

Quick-freeze a cat in a block of ice Wait a couple of days and then thaw the cat out. See if there's anything in all this talk about cryogenics.

Fill a soda bottle with gasoline. Jam a rag into the neck, and set fire to the rag with a match. Run like hell.

Why Boys Fudge Results

A boy will always have the strongest possible faith that, with proper lighting, sophisticated modern equipment, and carefully thought-out controls, he could probably come pretty close to getting the experimental results he was after. But a boy is always working under deplorable conditions and the best equipment he can get hold of is the second sweep of his watch and the make-do standard measure whose end points are the top of his head and the tip of his outstretched forefinger. Consequently, a boy isn't fazed if his experimental results are light years away from what he was after. A boy in fact has the very highest tolerance for inexactitude, error, and negative evidence, and he will always be willing to correct for it by going back and making allowance for wind conditions, temperature, and give, or simply forging ahead on the assumption that minor technical problems can be worked out later.

When a boy gets into the applied sciences, and particularly when he applies himself to engineering, he will always insist, despite all evidence to the contrary, that his knotty-pine shelves are roughly on a par with the Great Pyramid at Giza and that the problem has to be that the floor wasn't level or the lumberyard sent him one-by-tens rather than one-by-eights. When a boy has crafted a set of shelves or, in one of his more manic phases, an entire weapon system or a whole economy and not only does it not work but it refuses to be made to work and in the meanwhile it soaks up a whole lot of loose money, a boy will always develop a strong sentimental attachment to it. He will even go so far as to designate it a noble experiment, and he will proceed to enshrine it in a museum or make it a required course for freshmen. Still believing that deep down there is nothing seriously wrong with it, he might also base his re-election campaign on it and, later, by reconstructing its entire environment, finally get it to the point at which it at least emits a few promising sputters.

Boys and Banner Headlines

The kind of news story a boy really likes begins with a dramatic and unforeseen event as a result of which regular programming is repeatedly interrupted for bulletins and updates and Dan Rather is caught off guard and shuffles papers for several seconds before he realizes that he's on camera. Ideally, the dramatic and unforeseen event illustrates once again how incredibly vulnerable the peace and security of the world are to fanatics, crazies, misunderstandings, and human error. As the story develops, it provides strong evidence in support of a boy's favorite theories about Soviet opportunism, American impotence, British ineptness, and French cynicism, and it gives him an opportunity to sound off about what he would do if he were the President, Mr. Gorbachev, or the hostage spokesman. If all goes well, the world totters on the brink of total annihilation for a week or two. (Though a boy has nothing against a Falkland Islands crisis exactly, a Falkland Islands crisis will always have a Masterpiece Theatre or *Mouse That Roared* quality that a boy could live without; a boy always prefers at least a distant spine-chilling glimpse of nuclear winter.)

A boy's interest in a big news story begins to wane at the moment at which the march of front-page events slows down and, if he's going to continue with the story at all, he is going to have to do a whole lot of background reading in alien faiths and ideologies and he will have to put up with a substantial measure of ambiguity about CIA, KGB, and Mafia involvement, and instead of seeing the truth more clearly, he is going to risk losing sight of it altogether. By the time the ticker-tape parade occurs and Congress is debating whether or not to name a permanent holiday after the event, a boy has gone back to his Robert Ludlum novel and couldn't care less.

Boys and Television and the Movies

A boy is always at a real loss to explain how it is possible for him to have gotten so much pleasure out of and killed so many burdensome hours with television and movies that he holds in the utmost contempt. What a boy, in his haste to condemn, sometimes forgets is that the contempt is mutual. Moreover, television and the movies would quickly have to get a whole lot better if, on his third and most desperate combing of the local listings, he stuck to his original conclusion that there is nothing on and nothing worth going to see and if he got down *King Lear* or *Madame Bovary* from the shelf instead of getting it into his head that, if he really steps on it, he could not only make the 9:05 Sylvester Stallone at the mall but he could still be back in time to catch almost the whole of *Hawaii Five-O*. In defense of boys, it should be said at least that it never entered their minds to think of television and the movies as anything other than entertainment, or "something to do," or something to get into as a potentially glamorous and lucrative second career, and they have also never asked much of television or a movie other than that it contribute to their general fund of knowledge in such a way that, whenever they get into a game of *Trivial Pursuit,* they can dazzle the competition by calling up, with no effort at all, the brand name of the refrigerator in the Kramdens' kitchen in *The Honeymooners*.

Boys and Poetry

When once every second decade or so a boy comes face to face with a poem and, in a spirit of hardihood and adventure, makes an effort at wrestling the thing to the ground, he is usually confirmed in his prejudice that a really honest and straightforward person with something to say about immortality would just *say* it and not drag in a whole lot of irrelevant stuff about nightingales and grass. A boy also finds that he is usually able to express the complexities of *his* inner life simply by underlining the passages worth going back to in *Iacocca* and in Charles Schwab's *How to Be Your Own Stockbroker*. Occasionally, though, a boy will have a moment of such intense feeling and such heightened consciousness that he will borrow a pencil and he will ask the bartender for a couple of dry cocktail napkins and he will actually try to compose a verse or two of his own, and he will even get a couple of words into it and be quite pleased with himself until he realizes that he is at a loss for a rhyme for "a young lady from Liverpool."

When the afflatus passes, a boy will for several hours talk to himself and maybe to his dog and to any available girl in forsooths, harks, and who-goes-theres, and he will also feel great frustration at not having expressed his insight in the simple, forceful language and concrete imagery he heard so clearly inside his head and with which he was going to teach a couple of skeptics a lesson. Boys are in fact never entirely sure that poetry isn't the vocation they should have gone in for rather than dentistry or sportswear. They believe that, as poets, they would have been able to wear slovenly and outlandish clothing, their difficulties with spelling and grammar would not have been held against them, and, because poems tend to be on the short side, if they could just have learned a couple of the basic tricks and gotten over their writer's block, they would have been able to knock one out every couple of days without the job's seriously cutting into their handball schedule.

What a Boy Wishes for When He Blows Out All the Candles on His Birthday Cake

Total dominance and power

Some kind of cologne or pheromone ointment that would make him completely irresistible to women

World peace

Five million dollars, tax-free

The truth about who masterminded the Kennedy assassination and how they got away with it

To discover someone really original and to be her personal manager and lover

To do something so remarkable that the editors of *Time* magazine would unanimously vote him Man of the Year

Ten more good years

Another inch

How Boys Cheat Death

The way a boy sees it, death is an inescapable biological process—specifically, a breakdown in the oxygen cycle—by means of which, at least in the higher life forms, species have survived and prospered at the expense of individuals. It is characterized by inactivity, unresponsiveness to stimuli, and repeated chronic lapses of attention, and in all of these respects it is rather reassuringly like a boy's everyday life. Death is also, from a boy's point of view, a stunning excuse for not calling, not showing up, not shaving, and not doing anything about the way the front door squeaks; in fact, it is so unarguable an excuse that, if it is properly capitalized on, it has to afflict only an occasional drinking buddy or tennis partner in order to justify changing one's mind and not going to the dinner-theater production of *My Fair Lady* after all. On a day-to-day basis, death is also largely lacking in serious long-term consequences since, once you've counted to ten and taken a rest on the sidelines, they will usually let you back in for the second half. Boys, as it happens, will also from time to time catch a fleeting glimpse of utter dark oblivion, drear non-being, and the absolute extinction of self. In other words, they will catch a glimpse of the real existential horror of death behind the propaganda and the sympathy-card sentiment, and then they will sit up in bed in the middle of the night in a cold sweat. This is why, though boys court trouble and woo disaster, they will, finally, prefer only to flirt with death. Besides, however much a boy likes to have a scrape or a brush with death every once in a while, it will always be chiefly to remind himself that he's not just living, he's living it up.

Why Boys Believe That They Deserve One Last Chance, and What They Would Do if They Got It

Boys know that so far they have been a terrible, terrible disappointment to just about everyone. They've let people down. They've done next to nothing to inspire confidence. They also know that time is running out and that they have a great deal to make up for—specifically, the unreturned phone calls, the transparent lies, the sullenness, the not being there, the confusion, the muddle, the second balcony seats behind the pillar, the whole rotten mess. Boys are absolutely certain, however, that the standards they set for themselves privately, however little evident in their behavior, are immeasurably higher than any standards set for them by wives, girlfriends, and probation officers; and they are also absolutely certain that if they just put their minds to it and rallied their energies in a disciplined, grown-up way, they would make everything right once and for all. They would be saved from having to say "I'm sorry" because they would do more than just pay off debts, they would spread joy and peace of mind wherever they went, and they would also, in the process, finally realize their limitless potential and redeem themselves and perhaps their imperishable souls.

Why, then, don't boys act?

Boys don't act for the simple reason that they are waiting for the right moment; and, for boys, the right moment is always the last minute.

A boy wants to please his wife, his mother, his girlfriend, his other girlfriend, the cleaning lady, and even the solicitor for his college alumni fund, but he wants to do it dramatically. He wants to have two strikes against him in the bottom of the ninth, and he wants, for all practical purposes, to have been given up on. He would not even mind if a few shoes and ashtrays were thrown at him. Then he would come from behind with a miracle save and he would snatch victory from the jaws of defeat. A boy may even pull this feat off. He has the requisite optimism, the good heart, the inexhaustible supply of good intentions, the charm, the humor, the one nice suit, the couple of bucks in cash, and several major credit cards. In addition to his bravado, he also has an absolutely irresistible false modesty; and this is why, when he really has his back up against the wall and everything seems to hang on his next move, he will shuffle his feet, he will wipe his brow, he will take a deep breath, and he will mutter, half to himself, half to the universe at large, "Well, here goes nothing."